Praise fo

'... I found the Turkish players
improve themselves. They had a great desire to be successful
and to prove that Turkish players were up there with some of
the best of the World's footballers...'

Graeme Souness

'B & B is that rare type of book: honest, heartfelt, sensitively
told with a story that cuts across both romance and football.
It shows, incontrovertibly, that the beautiful game can be a
common language across cultures.'

Cool Publications

B&B describes the actual events that were to unfold from an
Englishman's chance encounters - firstly, with a professional
footballer; and secondly, with the woman who would later
become his wife. Both from the Islamic (Muslim) dominated
country of Turkey.

The book is an interesting interpretation of differences
between cultures, religions and people - but where true
friendship, admirably assisted by the language of 'football',
overcomes all barriers.

'B & B skillfully intertwines the three central themes of
football, human relationships and religion in a work, which is
an entertaining and alluring read.'

Minerva Press

Football is not a religion, but it certainly is a common language between like-minded individuals across the world.

Adrian Stores

Features in this work reference to more than twenty professional football clubs including: Manchester United, Manchester City, Leeds United, Blackburn Rovers, Chelsea, Rochdale, Galatasaray, Fenerbache, Stockport County and much more besides.

Adrian Stores was born in Littleborough, Lancashire. Educated at more schools than is easily recalled, he graduated from Portsmouth Polytechnic and later a Masters at Sheffield University. Brought up around Hollywood.........Hollywood, Stockport (England) that is. He is a supporter of Stockport County FC. He has always retained an interest in sport, leisure and tourism. He has acted as Chair to the Chartered Institute of Marketing's specialist consultancy group for these sectors. He now runs a marketing consultancy in his hometown whilst retaining an interest in all things related to Turkey and the game and business of football.

B&B

**Friendship
and
Football
beyond frontiers**

A real story

Adrian Stores

Copyright © Adrian Stores 2002

ISBN 0-9544457-0-8

This paperback edition 2003

Published by:

Acrobat Consulting & Marketing Limited
Marion House
62A Stockport Road
Cheadle
Stockport
Cheshire
SK8 2AF
ENGLAND

www.acrobatonline.com

Printed in Great Britain for Acrobat Consulting & Marketing Limited.

B&B: Friendship and Football beyond frontiers

A fascinating insight into another world.

The Author refers to actions, which are not commonplace in our Western World, but are gestures made from within a different type of friendship than many of us have had or could ever experience.

A recommended read for anyone interested in different cultures, romantic tales and the power of football.

B&B: Friendship and Football beyond frontiers is a real story.

B&B: Friendship and Football beyond frontiers

A real story...begins

The Home Fixture

1

"Ibne" is Turkish for a gay person, or so I am led to believe.

I have never had any homosexual tendencies to my knowledge.

These three months were about to change my outlook on life and respect for fellow humans, irrespective of race, colour, religion, or class.

My personal behaviour did not change and no, I didn't become a gay man, but the events that unfolded illustrated the power of friendship and bonding, which can prevail between different cultures.

2

Don't you just hate it when an author recalls the precise date and time of day of a life event?

I remember, that despite how much I enjoyed reading 'Fever Pitch' it made me wonder how Nick Hornby had the audacity to recall precisely the actual day on which each instance occurred.

Though I suppose it's different when you've got a Rothmans Guide or whatever to remind you of noteworthy fixtures.

You might have guessed I know a little bit about football.

Not an addict, but simply another supporter in the world of sport which some people blasphemingly call 'our religion'.

Well here begins my tale, which is superbly (...... if I say so myself) led into by reference to:

a man,

football

and religion.

Though there's much more besides.

Anyway I can't remember the actual date that this story begins, but Bilal Aksoy came into our lives sometime during the week of Monday 9th June Nineteen Ninety Seven....I think?

Actually the Turkish don't make a great deal of surnames so from here on in he's Bilal.

We were somewhere in the Otel Nazar. A quaint, probably 2ish star residence in Kusadasi. I had been frequenting this establishment for the last eight years.

Amazing, some might say. I think so.

Steve took me there the first time on a 'lads' holiday'.

I remember (so the brain does still function at times) he recalled that he had continued visiting the Hotel year after year, after year.

I said that I couldn't possibly keep returning as I'd enjoyed the previous holidays in common resorts of Corfu, Crete, Zante and other bits of Western Europe. Now it's my turn to blaspheme! Imagine what a few of my Turkish acquaintances would say if they knew that I, "Ady Abi" (that's me, literally Ady big brother) had visited a land under the auspices of the Hellenic Empire. You see not all Greeks and Turks see eye to eye. You know, the strength of ill feeling stemming from historical conflicts. The more vociferous might even describe them as the old enemy, but as Bilal said to me "who are you kidding Abi?....

The Greeks have a total population of 10 million, whilst we have this amount, maybe more, in Istanbul".

So I guess it's a somewhat mismatched encounter though I dare say there is another side to the story. The struggle continues AKA Cyprus to the very day.

Anyway, here I was again, hopping on a plane from Ringway (the old name for Manchester's airport) to visit not only Turkey again but good, old, Otel Nazar.

Shall I tell you where the name comes from?

No, I'll save that till later and get on with the storyline. I had heard that there was a professional footballer in the family, perhaps from Metin (this translates to Martin in English). He's Bilal's younger brother ("Metin kardes").

I hadn't really clicked who was related to who and the complexities of family relations, but nevertheless he arrived .....Bilal, that is.

I recall (see I'm getting the hang of it now) he stretched out of an arriving taxi. They seem to be mainly yellow. And was addressed by the customary hugs and kisses to both cheeks....on the face that is......which are reflex actions when a fellow, Turk (a friend that is) meets one another.

Not personally one to shy from such a visitation, I normally loiter to meet a contact with a humorous quip or the basic "Merhaba" (that's hello).

I'm pleased that this book will double up as a Turkish phrase book as well as a recollection of my life.

On this occasion, I hung back.

In fact I did more than this.

I continued with my socialising but did not go over to make my introduction.

It was probably self-conscious on my part, as for the next hour or two I remember constantly seeing him from the corner of my eye. I deduce now that I probably wanted to be more involved.

Yet I always knew he was there!

Bilal sat on the settee (no, I haven't learnt such essential Turkish words) and was deep in conversation with Apo (his father and a Partner in the Hotel this year) and Oner (the other Partner and a friend from the Village).

Kusadasi is not the Village, that's later.

Kusadasi is a cosmopolitan port town on the west coast of Turkey facing the 'enemy's' Samos.

I now tell the story that tourists flock to this Town with intentions of buying the splendid jewellery, leather or carpets found in its bazaar. The Yanks get off the huge cruise ships to spend their hard-earned dollars in such a way. Why couldn't I have followed this precedent and returned to our Island with such goods, rather than the professional footballer I was soon to adopt?

I'll tell you why. Because this would be the shortest story ever. An exaggeration but you get the point. Anyway I don't regret the times which are to enfold from this on the spur encounter.

Eventually, I left the dining area and traversed to the gents. He caught my attention or perhaps I caught his. I guess my name had come up in Apo's and Oner's conversation as I wasn't just another holidaymaker, with my track record of appearances.

We looked at each other and I said

"Merhaba".

He returned the word with a friendly smile.

Two more occasions occurred later in the evening when the same choice greeting was uttered from our mouths simultaneously. Hardly the longest conversation, but I was somewhat restricted by my lack of fluency. Imagine a script with one fat Englishman and an athletic foreigner (guess which one's which. No it's too easy!) meeting, maybe four times within the space of four hours, with merely hello, hello, hello, hello, hello, hello, hello, hello to utter.

The phrase, gibbering fool, is one, which now springs to mind.

Anyway this is how I first met Bilal, without whom there would be no story.

3

The Otel Nazar was being rented for one year by the Partnership.

A money making scheme was the intention, but nobody would begrudge this challenge if you knew of the upbringing.

Oner and Apo and indeed Bilal evolved from Albanians.

They are Turkish by birth but have an ancestry rooted in an Albanian province of Yugoslavia.

I think they or their families must have been immigrants to Turkey.

They now, outside the holiday season, live in a village (the Village) called Yeniköy that I believe translates as 'new village'.

It's about forty minutes by car from Kusadasi.

Oner tells how he sat beside his late father's (Saban was his name, now the name of Oner's son) bed and watched him die because the family had no money to pay for the medical care needed.

I have since learnt that it was cancer, so maybe cash would have merely prolonged the inevitable. I'm talking from my own experiences with my beloved grandfather, Bill Stores and recall the continuous trips to chemotherapy to no avail.

Oner followed up this potentially earth-shattering experience with a promise to better himself and have the necessary wealth to survive in this cruel world. He told me once how he went to University and lived in his car, a Tofas (Fiat to you and me) to afford his education. He's since had key appointments in the hotel trade and is now a Partner with I hope (Insallah) a prosperous future ahead.

How does a poor immigrant become a Partner one might well ask?

Apo was the finance behind the scheme and as a former landowner, agriculture I believe, sold his territory to support the endeavours of his friend.

This is the first time when I shall refer to actions, which are not commonplace in our Western World, but are gestures made from within a different type of friendship than many of us have had or could ever experience.

Eventually, the subject was broached.

"Can you let Bilal play football in England?"

Oner must have asked the question as Apo can't speak much English. Even less than I Turkish. But why should he with his life so far?

Never one to promise something that I can't deliver, I said, "I will try".

To many this could be seen as the impossible, but at least I had a head start with Steve [Steve Bellis - of whom I earlier referred] working for a club in my hometown, Stockport.

With the background from which my Turkish friends came, it soon became apparent from their ramblings that by securing a position for Bilal in England, there would be greater opportunity for him to increase his earnings.

In Turkey, outside the big four football clubs, Besiktas, Fenerbahce, Galatasaray and Trabzon Spor, a player has to be seen to do something different to progress.

This 'career-move' was thus based on PR (public relations for those of you outside marketing careers) in such tabloids as Yeni Asir; and a potential transfer back to one of these four.

I believe that there was probably a belief that he would get Ravanelli type wages, though I didn't let go of my opinion that this was a somewhat ambitious myth and communicated so at every available opportunity.

I didn't really talk any further with Bilal at this time, though it had been prearranged that he would accompany me in our drive back to Adnan Menderes, the airport in Izmir further North.

This journey was to comprise of chatting about international players currently in England that we would both know. DeMatteo, Vialli and Gullit (Chelsea), Juninho (formerly Middlesborough) and others which I can't quite recollect.

Football is not a religion...... but it certainly is a common language between like-minded individuals across the World.

Bilal was 23, I was older.

4

I returned to 'terra firma', Stockport in fact. There was a delay on leaving Adnan Menderes, but from what I can recollect in conversations with Pam, my girlfriend at the time…it was a sound holiday.

She had joined me for the second week of my vacation. A well needed extension following on from Steve's 'stag week' with thirteen disciples. Say no more!

Bilal wasn't central to our conversations, though I do remember Pam asking inquisitively,

"Do you think you'll be able to organise a trial?"

I didn't know, but knew Stockport County would be my first port of call the following week.

I rang Steve Abi, on the Tuesday and discussed life in the week previous when he'd returned home and I had stayed.

The consensus was that all the lads had had a great time.

The beauty was that we did not all have to follow 'the messiah' (Steve) but had been able to do our own thing. Naturally, peer groups developed with biases to tanning, excursions or drinking. I opted for the latter party. Not because I was the proverbial 'Brit. Abroad', but through a knowing of having seen a lot of what Kusadasi had to offer and a natural desire to let one self go outside the routine of work.

Why did I refer to Steve as the messiah?

I have not done so before.

Perhaps, because there were many who admired his patter and role in football (an aspiration of many a man and boy).

To me he was just a mate. A good one at that, and I

have to confess there probably was a bit of me which envied his career in professional sport - as Marketing Manager for Stockport County.

I mentioned to Steve about having met a Turkish player. He was interested to know more, but accepted my brief introduction. Our conversation ended with a promise to see what he could do, which I knew would mean an 'out of hours' chat with the Manager.

I heard nothing for a week, so continued my enquiries with the Club relentlessly.

I had made the acquaintance of Davey Jones (ex-Everton player and then Manager at County), and this was an opening, which I felt comfortable to develop at the right time.

...........................Then the bombshell.

I heard on the grapevine, Jones was leaving. Southampton, in fact, following Souness' departure to Italy, I think. Later, it was suggested that he would be taking the back room staff and maybe a player or two.

This was heart breaking as Stockport, my team, had an unbelievable season, the year before and had aspired to the heights of Division 1 via the automatic promotion route. Never again will the Club, in my view, witness such a spectacular season as I can constantly recollect the real dreams of beating Middlesborough, West Ham, Blackburn and Southampton in the Coca Cola Cup also.

As the Football Club's own marketing literature proclaims, County had come a long way since its reputation as the focus of 'music hall jokes'.

Some people blasted Jonesy for leaving, but I was a realist.

The guy had done much for the Club in his short reign and I for one could not bemoan him trying to better himself with a go at S'oton with the financial rewards that might bring.

So where did that leave me with the introduction of Bilal to football in England?

I couldn't do much.

So I sent a speculative letter to other teams in the North West.

The selection was based on driving times from my home, which would inevitably be his base.

The list included: Bolton Wanderers, Burnley, Wigan Athletic, Rochdale and Crewe Alexandra.

I also tried to speak to Jonesy at Southampton.

It was about this time that I thought I should let the 'Partnership', whom I had promised, know what I had been trying so I sent an update to Bilal at Otel Nazar:

1st July 1997

B. Aksoy Esq.
c/o Hotel Nazar
c. Turhan Blv. No54
Kusadasi
Turkey

Dear Bilal

Trial with English Football Club

I hope that you are well. This letter updates you on my work trying to get you a trial in England.

Stockport County Football Club were interested but the manager has now resigned. So I have sent your details to:

>**Bolton Wanderers**
>**Southampton**
>**Burnley**
>**Wigan Athletic**
>**Rochdale**
>**Crewe Alexandra**

I am waiting for their response. We shall 'keep our fingers crossed'. Good luck.
See you soon.

Yours sincerely,

adrian
-

Adrian Stores
Director

Simple and to the point.

As it transpired Bilal was never to read this letter as it would arrive after he had left his Country for a fresh challenge.

Needless to say none of the Clubs' Secretaries responded which is something I'd come to expect from this sporting world.

You see it strikes me as somewhat a clique and only recently have I been accepted as a worthy contributor.

I continued with my challenge and reminded Steve, gently of course, had he managed to explore the possibility of giving Bilal a chance.

Eventually, it was on one choice visit to the Club that Harry McNally entered Steve's office and I grasped the opportunity.

Harry had just joined as Chief Scout complementing a Managerial appointment of Gary Megson (ex-Blackpool Manager) and Mike Phelan (bags of experience with United and Eire).

I understand the sea-siders were none too chuffed by this poaching.

I guessed that Harry was somewhat taken aback by my directness and approach.

I recognised the man from a former life in football, but who wouldn't with his distinctive RAF style moustache.

If it wasn't for his attire, sporting a black Adidas tracksuit at the time, you would never have guessed his posture represented one of a person involved with the professional game.

7th July 1997

H McNally Esq
Chief Scout
Stockport County Football Club
Edgeley Park Hardcastle Road
Edgeley
Stockport
Cheshire
SK3 9DD

Dear Harry,

Trial Turkish Player

I am delighted that following my introduction of Bilal Aksoy to Stockport County Football Club you would like him to attend for a trial. The background to our approach has been explained to Gary Glendenning (letter dated 24th June 1997).

By way of introduction, I summarise his personal details:

Name:	Bilal Aksoy
Age:	23
Position:	Utility
	Preference, left/centre half
Skills:	Sound understanding of English game
Languages:	Turkish
	English
Present Club:	Aydin Spor

Currently sought after by various first division clubs in Turkey. I will arrange for Bilal to fly over as soon as practical and join you for training. Do contact me if you have any questions.

I ended with the usual round of best wishes and my signature above the title of Director. This time I also copied it to G. Glendenning to add more weight to it.

Harry, agreed and I set upon the task of notifying the Turkish Embassy that Bilal was required for a trial.

Steve Abi prepared a letter from the Club and I confirmed in writing that I would fund his flight and accommodation during his stay.

I typed both letters personally that day and faxed them to Oner on the 8th July and ECO British Consulate, Istanbul on the 9th.

Private and Confidential
7th July 1997

B Aksoy Esq
c/o Hotel Nazar
C. Tarhan Blv. No.54
Kusadasi
Turkey

Dear Bilal

Trial with Stockport County Football Club

I confirm that Stockport County would like you to attend for a trial for the football club. You should plan to arrive in England as soon as possible.
This letter may be shown to the relevant authorities in Turkey. I will pay for your flight and you will be provided accommodation at my home during your visit.
I hope that you will obtain the visa quickly as I do not want you to miss this opportunity. I look forward to seeing you.
With best wishes
Yours sincerely

adrian
-

Adrian Stores
Director

Merhaba,
Nasilsiniz? Eger Stockport 'a gelirseniz, beni arayin.
Memnun oldum.
Ady

In case you are wondering, the bit of Turkish scribbled on the bottom of the letter was my one and only attempt at communicating in writing to the natives over there.

Courtesy of plagiarising commentary from 'Aegean Sun': a freeby newspaper for the holidaymakers of Didim, Selçuk and Kusadasi.

It translates as something like: 'Hello, How are you? When you come to Stockport do drop in'.

This soon became a common 'piss take' by Bilal as the same words reappeared on other letters and even Birthday cards.

Well at least I try!

I did ring the Nazar to let Oner know the good news. I can't remember the response precisely…but they were pleased all right.

7th July 1997

TO WHOM IT MAY CONCERN

May I hereby confirm that Stockport County Football Club are prepared to offer Mr Bilal Aksoy a trial on the understanding that all accommodation and travelling expenses are met by our marketing consultants, Acrobat Consulting and Marketing Limited.

We would like Mr Aksoy to join us for our pre-season schedule, which commences on 9th July 1997 at the earliest opportunity and ideally no later than Monday 14th July 1997.

Please can you make the necessary arrangements to allow Mr Aksoy to take advantage of this opportunity. If you require any further information then please do not hesitate to contact me on 0161 286 8902 (office hours 9.00am- 5.00pm UK time).

Thanking you in advance for your assistance.

Best wishes and kind regards

SteveBellis

Steve Bellis
Marketing Manager

I made several telephone calls to Turkey to play my part.

The British Consulate was apparently only open in the mornings to receive applications for visas. Punters like Bilal had to wait for the remainder of the day to find out if they have been successful. What's more, Bilal had to fly to Istanbul to complete the exercise and Apo had to broach the subject with Aydin Spor.

So there were many complexities even at this stage.

5

About 10.30pm, Friday 11th July 1997 Bilal arrived.

I recall the girlfriend was not happy that she had to make the pick up from Ringway, at the time when many celebrate the end of another working week with pubs, clubs and whatever.

I had spoilt her Friday night.

You can guess, that I wasn't available.

Of all times for the Turk to arrive in my Country it was a double booking with a hospitality golf fixture at Wild Wood. A course somewhere down South. I would stay in London and get a taxi to Euston station at 5.00am.

Pam showed him a warm welcome. She even replenished the fridge with some bacon and pork sausages intended for his breakfast.

Dead useful for a Muslim!

But it's the thought that counts.

I can't tell you what happened at the airport, I wasn't there. However, I'm informed, she received a big hug and Bilal told how he was pleased to be back on the ground.

He hadn't flown before or even left his Country.

He had ended up getting a flight to Brussels and then another to Manchester.

Sabena had been his chosen airline.

Pam amusingly tells how Bilal tried to get in to the driver's seat not having time to acclimatise and realise us Brits drive on the left hand side.

He was driven back to my home where Pam put on the television and showed him my array of football videos.

'The World's Greatest Goals - From Bobby Charlton to Maradona',

'101 Great Goals',

'Kevin Francis - The Legend' to name but a few.

Apparently, 'County versus Burnley' became a favourite. A VHS of a game on 12th July, which we won 1-0.

You see from immediately landing in our Country he dedicated himself to the Mission.

A total focus on his aspiration to get a contract and help his family back home.

Commitment and study of the way the Club for which he was about to play pursued, before I returned.

6

There was no time to lose on my return from London.

Bilal and I met with the obligatory hug.

And, of course there was the odd 'Merhaba' or two.

We talked about his flight from Turkey and his arrival in our Country, but it was obvious that this was small talk and we soon addressed the serious subject of…football.

I had learnt that Bilal had been studying the Stockport County versus Burnley video. Just like a dedicated student preparing for an examination.

He had even viewed the highlights of the previous season video.

This meant that he now knew the players (both christian and surnames) and their strengths on the pitch.

Bilal recounted the formations 4:4:2 and compared the relative merits of each with styles of playing in other countries.

Apparently, Turkish teams had adopted the German's successful 3:5:2, presumably after the successes of World Cups and Euro '96.

It was always intended that we would visit Edgeley Park, the home of Stockport County, early on.

I suppose, I considered this some sort of baptism and wished to acclimatise Bilal to his imminent surroundings, as soon as possible.

I telephoned Steve Abi and arranged a rendezvous at the Stadium. A brief encounter at which we visited the club shop and stood on the hallowed turf. It's not like visiting United (Manchester, that is) but our homely ground reminded Bilal of life in lower divisions far away from our shores.

I was a proud tour guide.

Supporters of differing ages and backgrounds came to the ground, mainly visiting the shop as it was still close season.

One by one, I stopped them whether I knew them or not. At smaller clubs you do not know everyone, but recognise the faces. A common love results in a superficial bonding.

I introduced Bilal with pride as the latest import. He followed the footsteps of notable captures such as Louis Cavaco (Portugal), Martin Nash (Canada) and of course the man who first put County on the map, Danny Bergara (Manager- Uruguay).

The latter departed, supposedly after allegedly punching the Chairman (not a good career move!).

Some prearranged social activities were to follow.

The next day we were to drive to Lymm for a pub lunch. Steve Abi and his relatives and Bilal and me.

Immediately, Bilal was seen to be a different kind of person.

He took to the children.

First, Steve's girl Ashling and after, his brother-in-law's son, Danny.

Bilal was confident and caring.

I ordered a spicy starter and traditional English roast dinner, which he seemed to enjoy. I introduced Bilal to Anne (Steve's sister and wife to Gary- the brother-in-law).

The introduction comprised Bilal being a professional Turkish footballer who was on trial with Stockport County.

We never forget Anne's response,

"So Bilal, do you like football?"

Next, Steve's brother's (another Martin) fiancé, Tina,

had a surprise party organised at the Britannia Hotel in Offerton.

We all gathered in anticipation to a function room adorned by huge laminated posters of Tina in her youth.

I think it was her 21st Birthday.

After several blackouts and silence, Tina appeared at the doorway to a reception of party poppers, streamers and screams.

Everyone welcomed Bilal and wished him well. He mingled with ease and there was no falseness. Each person expressed genuine encouragement and hopes for Bilal's forthcoming test (the Mission).

It was a good evening.

Most memorable for the abundance of Turkish music.

Unplanned, but seemingly natural. Sezan Aksu et al (Turkish musicians) with accompanying dances.

Amazingly a large proportion of the guests had some affinity with Bilal's homeland and their dancing seemed second nature.

The dance floor couldn't have been more packed.

Turkey fever had hit Stockport.

Bilal enjoyed the party, politely rebuking the attention of a young admirer.

I was 'sarhos' (pissed), Bilal was not.

7

I soon learnt the rudiments of the Muslim faith. I even had empathy.

I knew that the Turks didn't eat pork - unlike my girlfriend. I understand that pig is perceived a dirty animal.

The stricter of Turkish Muslims did not touch alcohol or smoke.

Bilal observed these rules acidulously.

I discovered that the meat they ate had to be halal. I picked up that this was meat, drained of blood, and butchered by a person of Muslim faith.

Jewish, kosher, was not an acceptable alternative to Bilal.

The dinner at Lymm was an error. So were the earliest of meals, which I prepared. But later, we both established that halal was a must, so I regularly shopped at Rusholme or Levenshulme which are districts of Manchester with Asian populations and much halal. Otherwise, we ate out and had an Indian (not literally as he would probably get stuck in your throat) or Turkish cuisine.

I will never forget one of the rare occasions when I dared to leave Bilal to shop for food for himself.

You see I soon became the connoisseur of whether pork was included or non-halal ingredients.

He returned, dead chuffed with himself at having secured a monster pizza from Iceland (the supermarket store that is). I assisted the contents of the 12" box to the oven and then mentioned to Bilal: "You can't eat it!"

He went mad and claimed how on earth was he to know that the pizza contained meat?

I said really sarcastically: "Bilal, I know it's difficult,

but in England we find the title on the packaging is sometimes a give away".

I proceeded to point to the ginormous lettering on the box stating 'The Chicken Supreme'.

He picked off the diced pieces of chicken topping, one by one, as I tucked in.

We were advised by Suat, a nice guy, and proprietor of the ADA Restaurant, where best to find a mosque. Bilal was often seen, within our home, to read the Koran and pray with corresponding actions, which I did not yet understand.

We ventured to a mosque in Levenshulme. Stopping on several occasions to ask directions. Everyone seemed to know its location, but the instructions were not accurate. Ultimately, it was a C.A.B. which assisted us to find the destination.

It was the mid day, Jumar, session we tried to meet. This is a Friday and apparently one of the more significant ceremonies.

I pulled into the car park and we observed the mosque.

I remember thinking, was this the best our Country had to offer this Journeyman.

The building was an old structure, notable by its abundance of security mesh. There was no beautiful minaret adorning the facility as is commonplace in Turkey. I was embarrassed.

Apparently, this was a disused school.

We proceeded to knock on windows for signs of life.

Eventually, a middle aged, bearded man greeted us and we explained our purpose.

We entered the building.

To our left was a room with low washbasins. It is a requirement for the faith to clean their feet and other parts before a sermon. I peeked through the window to a hall where presumably the sessions were conducted.

The man, a kind person, welcomed Bilal and me and we entered the canteen area.

We sat at school desks, of the primary-school variety. Obviously, remnants of the venue's former life - education.

The man made us a cup of tea, in a saucepan, which was served in a plastic cup.

He handed Bilal a timesheet for the various preaching and started a conversation about the type of Muslim faith.

I began to understand (at least a little bit) that there were different types of Muslims. Bilal understood his explanation and I nodded.

Anyway we were welcome.

I was slightly fascinated.

I still visualise this fellow talking authoritatively about his faith whilst "chewing that stick".

Bilal later informed me that it was a ginger root and used to clean teeth?

We arranged to revisit at the next session. I did the honours as chauffeur.

It was suffice. Bilal returned on two occasions.

The latter, I feel guilty for, in that I sat in the pub opposite with two friends whilst Bilal prayed.

You see it was around 10.30pm one Friday or Saturday and I was following the usual weekend ritual of pubs.

Bilal and I often joked when on consecutive evenings I said that we would try something different.

One night we'd "visit a pub", and another "visit pubs".

I thought that this was variety, but he was simply

amused by this aspect of our culture.

Anyway, Bilal even managed to come out of the mosque with a Pakistani taxi driver, so we made our way home. The two of them chatted all the way home.

A quick, but common bonding.

I feel somewhat stronger than the supporters tribe at English football.

It was the same time that Sky promoted its' "Football is our religion" advertising. With Sean Bean. Bilal said that this was proper blasphemy and said "don't say that Abi!"

…if I ever was found to utter the phrase, even in jest.

Next we discovered that there was a large mosque in Rusholme. We were told the largest in Manchester.

We went one Friday.

I jumped out at an Asian convenience shop to ask directions and we were instructed on the way. We arrived around 1.00pm and I squeezed my car on to the grass verge opposite. The car park was full and this was obviously a full house.

Bilal went inside.

He was dressed casually, whilst the masses were in white robes or traditional dress. The mosque was over populated. Clearly, people of all ages, all males from my recollections, were praying within, but there was a notable overspill into the car park.

I watched through the fence and saw much kneeling and cupping of hands around the ear lobes. This was ritual. I humoured later that some men were pretending to be 'Bungle', the bear from the children's series called Rainbow. I meant a mimic of the hand cupping gesture. This was not a comment repeated, as despite it being an attempt to raise a smile, Bilal was not amused.

We left the mosque after about 30 minutes. He was clearly refreshed and pleased by the experience.

He recounted how people had looked at him as he clearly had lighter skin than the majority. But he was welcome.

8

I suppose the only 'minor' contravention of the Muslim faith was in relation to women.

Bilal had no difficulty, without trying, in attracting the opposite sex.

I learnt that he had left two (yes two!) admirers in his Country.

One who had given a ring, a sort of engagement, in Istanbul. She never rang him in England, but he let her parents' phone ring three times to let her know he was thinking about her. Apparently, her family did not think Bilal a suitable partner, so he had to be discrete.

The other, Meltem, was from Izmir, but she finished with him on his departure as she learnt about the competition in Istanbul. Nevertheless, her friend Kadriye rang regularly to say she was upset and to bridge the gap between the continents until his return.

I spoke to Kadriye once saying a few rude Turkish words jokingly. Bilal was supposedly rebuked with

"Can't you teach him anything good!" (at least this is the English translation of what I am informed was said).

The next time I sang.

Bilal and I had been walking back from an unusual expedition to a pub? He taught me "Ben sana asik oldum bir tanem".

This I found out was a love song, so I jested to cross the road, making gestations that Bilal was ibne.

Anyway I sang this song to Kadriye and she told Bilal I sounded nice.

He was tall, tanned, athletic looking and handsome, I am advised by female friends.

Each time we went somewhere, other than a pub remarkably, for a night out, he pulled! Not merely any young lady for the night but always the most beautiful in the venue. Whether it be a pub or nightclub, Bilal had normally attracted attention by his confident, arms out, figaro dancing on the floor.

Girl 1 (they shall remain anonymous to protect identities) was from the Efes Taverna, one Friday night in Manchester.

Bilal was taken there by me to meet some people from his homeland. I thought it could not be easy to settle so far from his Country on his first trip abroad. We sat together with a large plate of Turkish starters; I remember Sigara Borek at least.

Two tables down were a group of girls. We were later advised their earlier discussions were around a belief that we must be gay. Bilal's response was sharp and to the point, saying on their assumptions, they presumably were lesbians.

He succeeded.

The evening was not without other major incidents. Firstly, Bilal recognised someone at the bar as a familiar face.

He ventured over and was introduced by the Manager (an earlier acquaintance) to this boy. There had been such wind-ups before and so the boy did not believe that Bilal was from Turkey, never mind, Yeniköy.

Their respective Turkish identity cards were shown, with Bilal's birthplace highlighted and the two of them embraced.

It was miraculous that despite the distance Bilal had travelled, he had met someone from his village.

When we were being served at the table, I spoke my pigeon Turkish to the waiter. After several looks of bemusement he said in English

"I cannot speak Turkish I am Albanian".

Coincidence number two.

Meeting someone from his village was amazing enough and someone else from his 'original' land was incredible.

The rest of the night we met more and more Albanians. Virtually nobody could speak to me with their foreign tongues, so I communicated as I knew best and bought the beers!

Bilal retained an interest in the girl and I had a great laugh.

I remember, from the Albanians, Valentino and Nina; and Eddie by name. More by face.

Valentino was a waiter in Don Giovannis, Italian restaurant on Oxford Road. His past allegedly involved an appearance in the jails of Tirana for a family held belief contrary to the politics of the governing party in Albania.

He had the whispyissed moustache I had seen (unlike Harry McNally) and looked sophisticated.

Nina was his wife and very pretty.

Eddie was great. He spoke no English, just Italian and Albanian, of course. Eddie sounded like Ady so we bonded as friends.

Strange how such small similarities can instigate a friendship. We drank together, he gestured me on to the dance floor and I learnt "gosh nosht" (thank you) and "zooer" (cheers) in Albani.

My bar bill exceeded £90.

Bilal, the girl and I went home in a taxi around 3.00am.

We spoke in my lounge and then I made coffee.

She insisted that I stayed and talked, but I felt like a real gooseberry. Each time I went to make more coffee and tried to make a discrete departure she begged me to stay. Apparently, she liked my conversation….but she fancied Bilal.

On the occasions I returned from the kitchen, they parted as a young teen would on a father's arrival. I was embarrassed and headed for bed eventually.

I gave up my double and slept on Bilal's bed settee in the dining room. I heard footsteps as they made their way upstairs. After about ten minutes, Bilal returned to me. I exclaimed

"what's going on?"

He said

"Abi, we're getting close upstairs and she has said to me WOULD YOU MIND PUTTING SOMETHING ON?"

I said

"and……..".

"Well Abi, I've come downstairs for my leather jacket".

I howled with laughter.

Honestly, this is true. He had mistaken the request for a condom and taken the unclear question literally.

The event would never be forgotten.

The next day she invited Bilal and myself to a friend's wedding in Didsbury and said she would keep in touch.

Bilal rang several times.

I rang once. I spoke to her, but she never got in touch again.

She was an educated girl, but clearly this was a 'one night stand'.

Both Bilal and myself were surprised.

Girl 2 was found at Fridays nightclub and was a friend of my drinking partners, Little Al and Big Ian.

She returned to our home, but they didn't move from the lounge.

I made sandwiches for her cousin who sat talking to a neighbour on the wall outside. They left by taxi around 1.00am to Worsley.

The next day I discovered slices of bread and cheddar growing in the front garden. Obviously, not one of my better butties.

We got another taxi that night and the manager, a tubby Iranian from Cheadle Cars, told us the girl's boyfriend had been waiting for her at home on the drop the previous night.

Well Bilal was starting to understand the mentality of the type of English girl you can meet at a club.

Girl 3 was not so much a conquest.

We went out with Martin and Tina and their friends. After a few drinks in the Stockport Arms (a pub), I whispered to Tina to say to Bilal

"You have ….. kuçuk yarak" (a small dick).

This had the desired effect in that he rose to the bait and rebuked the suggestion.

I knew it would get a laugh and dent his confidence for a while. He offered to display his manhood, but everybody advised him that this was not the done thing.

We went to more pubs and a club called Luckies, then rounded the night off with an ample portion of fish and chips.

Bilal enjoyed this meal.

The first experience of this English tradition (with Grandma) was just about okay, but he learned and commented that the time to get most enjoyment was by eating it late and with mushy peas and curry sauce.

He walked behind the Town Hall with his latest conquest and proceeded to issue the chat up line

"I think it is about time that I show you".

It was not a notable success.

A week later we went to Mulberrys in Withington. This was to be the girl whom became his English girlfriend.

Again, he danced majestically as the wooing movements began.

Donna was ensnared.

She came to talk with me later that night to check out Bilal's age.

She was besotted. Her love life had not been memorable for the right reasons. She had been married to a guy in Brighton.

Donna, we often childishly called her "Kebab", was pretty in a long patterned red dress. We had many a day out with Donna. Sometimes Bilal stayed at her house in Reddish. It was good that he had two homes.

9

Wе lived in a terraced road in Cheadle, near Stockport.

A simple two up two down was the accommodation, but suffice for our football viewing and lives.

The house had no name, just 41.

It later was called either "Manisa" or "Bakirköy".

These were names of large mental hospitals in Turkey and were therefore appropriate similarities to the household of a crazy Abi and Kardes.

We watched football on Cable TV as often as it was available.

Sometimes up to three games an evening. We never got bored.

We even found a Teletext page on Channel 4 with Turkish results.

The situation became untenable for my girlfriend.

She said that it was because we were so close. Bilal and me that was.

I expect the final straw was when she had discovered the previous night we had been rehearsing all Bilal's celebratory dances to be used on the pitch after he had scored a goal.

Somewhat premature you might say, but we enjoyed it.

We even conjured up the odd chant from the terraces, such as converting the chart hit of D.I.S.C.O to B.I.L.A.L.

Hardly innovative, but good clean fun.

It is true that Bilal probably learnt very little from me during his stay.

I told him that to "turn on" had two meanings. Firstly, the light and secondly, the woman.

I think Donna got sick of Bilal saying
"Am I turning you on, sweety?"

I chuckled the only time when he appeared scared.
A loud volume came from supposedly outside.

As it transpired, Bilal had sat on the remote control for the television.

Not quite as daft as when I asked him if he'd seen the phone ......and it was in my hand!

I took him on a day trip to Morecambe. The purpose was to watch a pre-season friendly with Stockport County.

I taught him the "I do like to be beside the seaside....." song.

He couldn't remember the lyrics and merely groaned "this is rubbish song Abi".

We watched the game, County won 2-0 and then I took him to see the seaside.

I was flabbergasted, the coast in Morecambe was rubbish. We couldn't even see the tide.

Bilal laughed recounting Ladies Beach, Tusan and Long beaches back home in Kusadasi and said "em......very nice, Abi. But I think this is different! No sea, just side?"

Theresa, a single Italian lady was the neighbour. It became ritual that we danced on her wall on trips to and from the pub or pubs. We all became friends and on one visit from her Italian Cousin, I took them to the ADA Restaurant for a birthday treat for Bilal.

He had already spotted the Cousin before, sunbathing in the back yard from my upstairs bedroom window. We giggled like mischievous, schoolboys as we peeked at the scantily clad woman. Later, he went down to look over the fence and chat. I squirted him with talcum powder from above.

How old were we?

On his birthday, I told him that I was pleased an old friend from University would be joining us. She arrived at the Restaurant and sat next to Bilal. I had already warned the entire custom that she would come. In fact she was a stripogram.

He proceeded to be massaged with baby oil and be spanked with a horsewhip. He frequently announced his innocence and to one request from the girl performer said "I can't take my trousers off here. This is a restaurant, not the bedroom!"

Theresa took pictures. She later presented them in an album and he said "Thank you, but I think I cannot show these to my mother".

The stripogram gave Bilal a certificate for his pains.

We had much amusement during his stay.

Bilal drove once... but never again.

It had something to do with his not stopping at a 'give way' junction at a roundabout (Bilal called them "circles") and my dazed response.

We once went to a Ferrari garage, but I sensed we were found out, given our attire of jogging pants and T-shirts compared with all the other potential customers who were smartly dressed.

We agreed that this would be our life-style ...one day!

10

Bilal started to play football with Stockport County. He went training with the first team squad at a practice ground in Knutsford. I organised my timetable to allow regular attendance in the first week to check he was okay.

Football is a common language and certain players started to make him welcome. These started primarily with the other players from abroad, but as each day progressed more and more spoke with him.

I'm not sure if it's the shyness of the majority of the British ...or the fear of them having their own positions threatened?

He soon got known as "Big Turk".

Bish the Stadium Manager and kitman greeted him and provided training gear. He told how he was removed from Turkey, I think after a brawl.

Bilal was a natural athlete with a physique that echoed this fact. He was clearly the fittest of the bunch and whilst his early touches left something to desire was a 'true professional'.

I bought him some boots, Adidas Predator, as he only had moulded studs from Turkey.

After Wednesday of that week, Steve Abi was informed that perhaps Bilal - "the lad had set his sights a bit high".

Mike Phelan said this.

But an introduction to Sammy McIlroy was in the offing and Bilal was told to report for a game against Dundee from Scotland. He was to get the full ninety minutes at centre half.

My jealousy of Steve Abi was in abeyance.

I had been admitted to the soccer fraternity as I

conversed with stars, past and present.

Can you imagine sitting in my back yard receiving a call from Chris Waddle (manager at Burnley) or travelling around London in the taxi and speaking with John Deehan (Wigan)?

On learning that Bilal was wanted by Macc. Town, suddenly Gary Megson wanted to think again.

You can imagine him thinking, had he missed something in evaluating Bilal's potential. The excuse for his release was an abundance of centre halves - 5 or 6, I think.

Bilal played for Macclesfield. I thought well. Steve thought not.

I ran around the pitch with my Minolta 500 Si, snapping photographs of my brother in action.

It so transpired only 4 of the 36 came out, as I hadn't yet mastered moving shots.

This was to be a good piss take over the coming weeks between Bilal and me.

I was no David Bailey!

After the game I went to see Sammy who said he had been impressed.

I was delighted when he asked if Bilal could continue to train with his first team.

So he joined Macclesfield.

Richard Landon, the centre forward and former Stockport County striker was to take Bilal from Stockport to Macclesfield each day.

After one week I learned he would not be taken on as recently they had agreed to sign another centre half, from Stevenage. A distinctive player who wore a blue bandana.

Bilal had been rejected for an abundance of defenders at both Stockport and Macc.

Whilst all this was happening, behind the scenes I worked on the work permit application.

We tried a London firm, before deciding on a Manchester practice with links to Manchester United. Maurice Watkins was a partner - the legal voice at United.

We revisited all Bilal's life:

1996-1997	Aydin Spor	Professional footballer
1995-1996	Yeni Nazilli Spor	Professional footballer
1994-1995	Yeni Bornova Spor	Professional footballer
1993-1994	Altay	Amateur footballer
1989-1990	Hotel Golden Sands	Barman
1988-1989	Hotel Golden Sands	Work placement
1987-1988	Hotel Imbat	Work placement
1986-1988	Hotel Imbat	Work placement

It appeared a student oriented-placement with my Company, Acrobat Consulting and Marketing Limited would be his best chance.

He was not an International, nor in Europe, which are pre-requisites of the Home Office and FA.

Stockport College offered him a place on a GNVQ in Leisure and Tourism.

Ridge Danyers College in Cheadle would take Bilal on an NVQ in Sport and Recreation. We argued this would relate to his education back home as he was part way through a degree at Ege University in Izmir at Beden Egitimi Spor Yuksek Okulu (a College).

We couldn't track down any long lost relatives in Europe to assist his cause.

I was persistent and wouldn't take no for an answer! Next I got him into Rochdale Football Club.

This was to be his longest trial.

I always made it clear that I was not a Football Agent. Graham Barrow, the then Manager agreed to take a look. I found this man most sincere and after only a few days he said "the lad's got ability. If we were a bigger club I'd sign him now".

I liked his style.

Graham was frequently to be seen in a suit and managed the team's affairs often from the shelter of his office. I know from desperate attempts of trying to get hold of him he spent many hours on the telephone. When he did venture into sports wear he was to be seen showing a large "GB" on his tunic covering his portly figure.

I remember the first day I took Bilal into the changing rooms.

Nobody spoke.

I took matters in to my own hands and expressed my confidence by orchestrating the seasoned professionals to greet Bilal one by one - and to take Bilal 'under their wings'. An Abi/Kardes action.

Joe was the Coach and GB's assistant.

A dual job with physio responsibilities, as smaller clubs cannot afford such luxuries. Bilal said he thought that Joe's training was the best he had experienced in England. They trained on a primary school's pitch and I often watched, sat on an iron bench.

I recall on the second day seeing Bilal score a

tremendous goal from forty yards during a kick about match.

Bilal was now still "Big Turk" but also "Billy".

It made for much comedy with the calls as he played alongside "Hilly" at the heart of the defence.

I could see the potential of my brother. It was rare to find such a natural left-footed player for central defence.

Many of us travelled to Spotland, the home of Rochdale to watch Bilal.

Steve Abi, Gary, Martin (Tina's fiancé) and Tina, Valentino and Nina and Alex Abi a distant cousin of Bilal's from Birkenhead.

He came on as substitute against Preston in a pre-season friendly.

He did well.

The Manager was pleased.

I still watch the video to the very day.

His first real encounter of English competitive football. Even the supporters were impressed shouting "Come on Billy Axol".

I suppose this was close to his actual name?

The weeks progressed, 7 in fact.

I manipulated behind the scenes making contact with influencial people at Rochdale, the PFA and the Chairman.

It was a long trek to Rochdale every day on the M63.

On one day a new colleague of mine agreed to pick up Bilal from Worsley where another player, Nick had dropped him off.

The journey should have been 20 minutes. After 60, Chris rang to say she was lost. I jokingly raised my voice and said "My brother's a professional footballer.

He will be getting cold. Get in the car and pick him up".

She didn't see the funny side and was apparently close to tears. She eventually came to Bilal at the roundabout, off the slip road and after driving around it twice Bilal stepped out in to the road shouting

"STOP!"

She was a rubbish driver.

We even trained ourselves in the evening. I always started at an impressive pace, leaving Bilal in my tracks.

I actually used to be a runner.

But after 5 minutes I tired. I wasn't in shape. Then I walked and we laughed about it later.

Whether I was there or not conducting the training: both fitness and ball skills; Bilal often found children to kick about with.

This is not a common sight in the world in which we live with parents fears of paedophilia.

He was simply a genuine, caring gentleman in the truest sense of the word.

Bilal was requested to play against Barnsley reserves on Wednesday 13th August 1997. A team recently promoted to the Premier League, the outfit which play at Oakwell were giving a trial or debut to a Finish (I think that was his nationality!) goalkeeper, Lars Leese.

The surroundings were most memorable for the 'redness' of the stadium.

I expect Liverpool or United could be the same.

It was particularly noticeable in that the attendance was naturally low and the empty red seats were in abundance.

Malcolm Shotton (ex-Oxford United and Nuneaton Town) was in charge of the Barnsley team. I felt his constant sergeant major-like bellowing at the officials could probably be heard back in Lancashire.

In my pre-match chat with Graham he said Bilal was doing well in training and even if they got "stuffed" 5-0 he still had a chance of getting a contract. They did and he played badly.

The pressure to succeed in this one off examination was too much. Mind you I have no idea why Joe chose to play three at the back away from home. The entire team was ran ragged that cold September evening. Bilal had appeared on the teamsheet at number 6. It read "Axol Bilal".

Graham was not there but you could tell had a soft spot for Bilal. Nobody worked harder in training than his Turkish recruit. His generosity rewarded Bilal with a final chance.

Shrewsbury reserves away in the pouring rain.

It was The Pontin's League fixture on Wednesday 3rd September 1997 at Gay Meadow. No specific relevance to 'ibne' in the name.

Simply the home ground of Shrewsbury Town, nominated by some as one of the more scenic grounds in the Nationwide League.

Apparently as it backs on to the river, people on one side of the banks call it "Shrews…bury"

and the other "Shrows…bury".

Bilal was not listed on the teamsheet among the preprinted team.

In front of me in the stand sat a group of what I can only describe as public school like young girls. I gathered from their behaviour that their attendance at reserve team fixtures was a common event.

One wore a replica blue shirt with the name of Nwadike embossed. He looked to be a solid Nigerian at the heart of Town's defence. Indeed, I believe that he was the one which Bilal had a minor rumpus with in the combat of the game.

Bilal was substituted at half time. I didn't think he deserved to be.

Joe later asked me what I thought about his performance.

I bit my lip and said I would abide by his decision. Rochdale had come to an end.

We talked as we travelled to my mother's in Birmingham that night. Rebecca my sister was there. He was welcomed in to the family and football wasn't discussed.

We agreed one more try … at Doncaster Rovers.

We arrived at Doncaster after an introduction from Steve Abi to the caretaker manager, Mark Weaver.

He was excited by the prospect of a left-footed centre half, as Doncaster were towards the foot of the table and leaking goals every game.

Incidentally, Andy Thorpe, former captain of County was on trial in this arranged Pontins League fixture.

The administration of the club was run from portacabins. The place lacked atmosphere and apparently they were in financial difficulties.

I was led to believe that Bilal, the Turkish import, had featured in the evening paper.

Yet he did not play.

This was the first club which insisted on a Clearance Letter, and whilst I was told that Aydin Spor had given Bilal permission, this was insufficient for the surly Company Secretary.

We duly left the Club after completing the necessary paperwork for the FA and left Doncaster without a result.

The Manager would have let him play but the Secretary had experienced the wrath of the FA with a recent trialist from the West Indies.

Two weeks later we received a letter on official letter heading notifying us that

BILAL DID NOT HAVE CLEARANCE.

To some this might have caused disdain after all our valiant efforts.

I wouldn't have swapped the months and had no regrets.

Plans were made for Bilal to return home, to Turkey, and Apo made the arrangements for Bilal's imminent arrival with Aydin Spor.

Grandma showed the first real emotions since her husband's death as she embraced Bilal on his farewell.

There were no tears as Donna and I would be jetting off to join him two days later.

The Away Fixture

11

We arrived at Izmir's airport. The flight was delayed, so we had more beers before departure.

Donna helped me to choose a suitable fragrance in the duty free.

Chris, a colleague came to, on the pretence of work.

Apo met us on arrival and we journeyed to the Nazar.

Now the name (Nazar) literally means, a good luck stone with an 'eye'.

Sold to tourists by the thousand.

A friendly greeting as always ensued.

Bilal was not there.

The holiday was okay, not brilliant. I wanted to do my own thing rather than be the girls' tour guide.

On a particular day, Taner and Simon the barmen (boys really) took me to Yeniköy.

I met Oner's mum in her dwelling.

Beyond belief, a little settlement between hills, surrounded by Kurds picking 'pamuk' (cotton to us).

The houses were testimony to the old ages with old stone walling as we might find back home in the Yorkshire Dales.

The mother welcomed me and offered 'cay' (tea - in a small glass with a silver spoon and a saucer with two sugar lumps).

The circumference of the lounge was one settee after another, head to head. All were different colours - like furniture from the sixties. She would have won no prizes for decor, but the surrounds were welcoming.

I discovered that she was a diabetic, like my Gran. We nodded and smiled. No English could be spoken here.

Later I went to Bilal's home.

Only the mother was there. I mistakenly, tried to kiss her on the cheeks.

She refused.

This was too informal a greeting for the Muslims in this village, at least certainly the elder ones.

All were covered from top to toe as the traditional dress of these people.

She made me welcome with cay as we sat sock-footed in the main room.

She then brought me pictures of Bilal in his youth and I discovered that he had had a brother before Metin, also called Metin, who had been shot in an accident in the Village. Why had Bilal never mentioned this before?

She showed photographs of the girl in Istanbul.

I remember thinking I was glad that I had left Donna at the beach.

Then we left for Aydin to try and see Bilal at his football club.

I got the greeting right on leaving the Aksoy house (kissing the mother as an elder should be - that is first on the hand and then raising the same hand to touch your own forehead) and waved bye-bye.

12

We travelled to Aydin Spor and pulled up a dusty side road to the training ground and residential camp.

We met Bilal behind the perimeter fencing and were informed that he couldn't leave.

Apparently, the team had lost at the weekend and all the players had to stay in their rooms.

It was very different from professional football in England and I was saddened.

This was like PRISON!

We chatted briefly and left.

We met up with a Turkish 'tart' at the Hotel, Banu.

At least I was advised she was not a prostitute.

We also made the acquaintance with Fatih (what a name… imagine calling a son after the action 'to break wind'). He was the brother of the guy who accidentally shot the first Metin.

I had accompanied Donna around the Friday market and the myriad of bargains. Bartering was in abundance.

I really question the worth of shopping in England when I see the plentiful supply of goods, clothing and leather mainly, at a fraction of the prices, which we are used to. This was whilst we were waiting for Bilal.….as usual. It was a regularity, waiting for Bilal that is, which amusingly became known as B.A. time.

Bilal eventually came to the Hotel in Kusadasi.

Donna was aggrieved when he embraced me before her. But we were family.

Bilal asked if we could become blood brothers.

I shyly said I was worried about AIDS and refused the offer.

Everyone welcomed him and he was polite to all.

He danced to the Turkish music with women of all ages. Donna attempted to teach him line dancing which he mastered.

His highlight was a Michael Jackson dance. When the dancer slurs his feet without normal moves in a robotics fashion. I believe they call it 'moonwalking'?

He was a real star.

The short time together was fun.

Before we left for England, Donna, Chris and I sat and talked with Bilal at a table in the Hotel.

We began to recite humorous stories of Bilal's stay in our Country.

The reality of the adventure being over started to dawn on us all.

At one point I commented that we would be having a meal, the three of us, and Grandma, on my return.

I stressed to Bilal that of course, I would make sure that it was halal.

At this point I began to cry and the girls followed suit.

On the journey back to the airport, Bilal played all the songs from the charts; all of which had special memories for us all.

Men in Black
I'll see you when you get there
Missing You
I get knocked down but I get up again etc

Tears flooded down my face as I stared silently out of the window.

I can only assume the girls did similar; and I feel Bilal did in the front of the car alongside his father.

I had never seen Apo show emotion before.

He hugged us all and then father and son cried at the airport as we said farewells.

B ilal and Turkey could not be forgotten back home.

On arrival in England we learned that Sun Tours had gone bust.

This meant our Turkish-Albanian friends had no tour operator for the forthcoming season and a prospect of no customers.

They lost about £9,000, a lot of money over there. But eventually took over an alternative hotel, the Onat (literally, ten horses) and I became a Partner.

Steve Abi and I travelled again in November to check the venue.

I went in all thirty-three rooms and inspected, beds, shower curtains, balconies, cupboard handles, lighting and cleanliness.

It was a good hotel, better than the Nazar and on a secluded beach called Ladies Beach to the South West of Kusadasi.

We visited Aydin Spor stadium to watch Bilal in action.

It was reserves versus first team.

The Teknik Direktor (Manager) strolled around the turf shouting.

He reminded me of Danny Bergara.

Bilal started in the reserves, but changed at half time.

He had been struggling to get first team appearances, but still to this very day one of the coaches at the club says "why can't your friends from England return for every match?"

This quip is based around the fact that Bilal played out of his skin that day. We suspect for our benefit.

He concluded his performance by rising majestically to head in a cross for a superb goal and was mobbed by teammates.

We went down on to the pitch after the final whistle and I handed Bilal a Manchester City sweatshirt, which I had bought as a present.

You see his favourite venue visited in England was Maine Road (the home of Man City). It was a drab, draw against Tranmere Rovers, but it was the atmosphere which excited Bilal and the roar of such anthems as "City till I die".

He was clearly under pressure and marshalled away by the Teknik Direktor to the team coach, which would take them ….back to prison!

That was all I saw of Bilal on that trip.

15

Before we next met, there were only telephone calls.

Regular at that….. at least from one of us. You can guess which one was better at keeping in touch by the message left on my answer phone…..

"Hello, Abi. Why you didn't call me? I wait for your call; you know your little brother, kardes. I will call again maybe tomorrow, maybe Friday. I miss youooooooo! See you when you get there……………You are ibne, Abi."

16

I travelled over next on 28th December.

The purpose, to visit the Hotel and show the Partners how I'd been getting on arranging to market the accommodation for the forthcoming holiday season.

Apo and Oner picked me up at the airport after a two hours delay from Istanbul. You see outside of the summer, flights do not go direct from Manchester and we must change in Istanbul.

Why do so many think of Istanbul as the capital city?

It is actually Ankara which has this status.

Bilal was there to.

He greeted me donning his Manchester City sweatshirt and said he would see me tomorrow, after training.

I thought, maybe B.A time?

We journeyed the 30 minutes trip, stopping outside Selçuk for 'corba' (soup). At least, that's what they had.

I had a beer.

It was really a 'home from home abroad'. In fact, this became the strap line for the brochure that I wrote to promote Otel Onat.

All my friends worked in the Hotel. Metin, Lee (actually Levent), Simon (Sinan) and Taner.

All resided in Onat during the winter, except Lee who we suspected of being a pimp with Ukranian girls. Anyway he had a gun. I was petrified; not merely because of Metin's (the former brother) experience but because you don't get a second chance if you make a mistake with this weapon.

At this time of year, the Town is deserted. The

municipality take no care of the beaches which look unappealing dressed in litter and seaweed. Life at Ladies Beach for us meant huddling around a four-bar, electric fire with copious cups of cay; and backgammon for entertainment.

A prostitute came to book in one night. She said she wasn't, but I knew better. Despite, my lack of appreciation of the Turkish language I could tell that her sob stories were too far fetched. I leant behind Sinan's back and whispered to Metin

"Oh... so sad".

He pissed himself laughing.

Apparently within the depths of the conversation about her pitiful life, my whisperings had been synchronised with her commenting about how she had broken her mobile telephone.

I got bored and went to bed

...ALONE!

I said

"iyi geceler" (good night).

She was shocked by my Turkish; and both she and the lads encouraged me to say something else.

I was tired and ready for my pit and rebuked

"Aminakorum" (which apparently means go put your dick in the pussy).

Highly appropriate, don't you think, even if it was a reflex response and not really a comment thought through.

Anyway it made my friends laugh.

Bilal visited every night.

I decided to make a video to promote the Hotel. It still remains an aide-memoir to the folk over there.

Trying to find a cameraman or even a camera was a joke. Yet we discovered one who we hired for a day

72

and he filmed me, talking pigeon English introducing the resort on New Year's eve 1997.

We filmed everyone, Taner, Oner, Apo, Metin, Sinan and Levent.

We couldn't stop laughing at the poor show we all made of pretending to be actors.

I orchestrated the filming of the accommodation, Ladies Beach, Bird Island, the Grand Bazaar and we ended with a trip to Emperor Bar where Fatih was head barman.

"He used to be bodyguard to a Turkish Admiral" was my commentary on the video.

Believe it or not the year was seen in to the chorus of 'jingle bells' … and we all waved sparklers moronically.

Well, this was after the customary belly dancer had left.

I concluded the video by introducing Bilal who said

"I've played for Stockport County, Macclesfield and Rochdale and so I know what the English people like. I promise you will enjoy my Country".

This clip was filmed to the backdrop of the Turkish flag, whilst I commented in front of the Union Jack.

We watched the video in Yeniköy after a superb feast prepared by Bilal's mum.

Eight of us sat bare footed and ate chicken stock soup, a delicious chicken and rice Albanian dish and borek.

The Mayor of the Village came which made me feel important.

At first the video cassette wouldn't work, so a phone call to a supposed technician told us to heat up the cassette recorder by the fire.

I had my doubts about the course of action, but it

worked and we watched, about sixty minutes, and laughed.

Later the Mayor told how one day after Apo had first bought the electric fire, he lay with his head on a mattress, close to the fire.

Apo woke to discover his head felt very hot and responded by moving the mattress around to try and avoid this sensation; rather than simply moving the pillow to the opposite end!?

The story had everyone falling about in hysterics.

The elders went to the mosque later that evening and the boys (me included) went to the Tea House (literally, cay ev).

It was incredible to think that people spent their leisure time in this way.

No television, just cups of tea and conversation - but they were happy.

A most memorable incident was that I saw the mirror image of the Turkish flag .....the simple moon and star.... in the sky as I strode the cobbled lanes.

My friends explained that this was how the Country's flag evolved when this vision was reflected in a post-battle pool of blood back in time.

I left Yeniköy with a pottery decanter (hand made) and the promise of a head dress for the day I get married.

This would be for my wife.

The next day Bilal took me to Izmir to meet Meltem and Kadriye.

We played tenpin bowling which I won and sat beside the river playing first OK and then Backgammon.

Kadriye had many phone calls to her mobile, mainly as a result of me playing the fool. It wasn't funny when we learnt that she awaited news of her brother who was in hospital following a car accident.

We constantly laughed at the numerous times which I saw the sign for Manisa.

A simple life but so much fun with my new found friends.

We concluded Ramazan with Iskender Kebab and a glass of Coca Cola.

Then I returned to the airport to fly home, via Istanbul.

I booked into the Hotel Inter in Beyazit, a rough quarter near the Bosphorous. I was back with Pam and so hunted the shops for some boots ("hippy chick" ones) and a handbag for Grandma.

I stayed up at the bar in the Hotel that night. The Steward, another Metin, kept telling me how he enjoyed getting "pissed as an elephant".

Baileys and Jack Daniels was his favourite mix.

I was promised an early morning call, but unsurprisingly it never materialised.

I found the Steward slumped over a chair when I awoke.

The Taxi Driver ripped me off on the journey to the Airport.

I even saw a sign for Bakirköy.

The experience was coming to an end.

I had come full circle, both home and away.

The months would never be forgotten and nor would Bilal.

I did however sit next to a beautiful Turkish girl on the airplane.

17

The girl was called Bilge. Pronounced "BILLGAY".
It was a strange sort of conversation, when it started
- instigated by me.

Principally, because she spoke little English and my
Turkish is "bobbins".

We sat and I glanced occasionally her way. She was
young and had a pretty face. I felt paternal to her.
Weird you might think on first meeting, but a virgin
flight and first journey from her homeland was enough
to endear me.

She was to become... the second B, in this tale.

We communicated via finger-pointing in our
respective English - Turkish, Turkish - English
dictionaries.

Just as in Efes Taverna, with the Albanians, language
could be overcome by body language and chemistry.

The real ice-breaking was my asking her if we could
smoke in these seats. She asked the stewardess who
responded negatory. So we both traversed to the rear of
the plane to the smokey section. Both inhaled, despite
her having given up. Already I was a bad influence, but
it was her choice. We met other folks and engaged in
chat.

Oh, I didn't tell you, on arriving at Ataturk Airport,
after much waiting and queuing, I was advised that my
seat had been sold.

The alternative was to fly to London and get a
shuttle to Ringway.

A number of us suffered this inconvenience, but
despite the cock-up we still say to this day

"Cok Tesekkur Ederim Turk Hava Yollari".

Literally, Thank You Turkish Airlines, without which

I would not have met Bilge.

We exchanged addresses and telephone numbers.

She wrote on a scrap of paper taking details off the letter she had received from her family. She was going to be an au-pair for two years.

I gave her my business card.

She presented me with a metal lighter.

I tried to reciprocate with my personal stereo.

She already had one so I resorted to 'worry beads'.

I remember Bilge said to me that she had heard that English people were cold, but having met me she felt reassured. I was proud.

I helped her to carry her bags off the plane, then she scarpered off to meet her new family, whilst I tried to work out how I could get back to Stockport.

Around twelve of us had suffered the same fate. However, the commaradery was great as we sat in a circle on the lounge seats and bought drinks and smoked to our hearts content. The tactics came to play, on how to get home, by pleading with the supervisor at Heathrow, to be moved up the Stand By list.

I negotiated well and helped a girl (maths teacher from Sheffield) to board also.

My generosity was further extended by buying rounds and letting the others use my mobile phone to give constant updates to their families whom were waiting up north.

We arrived at Manchester and said our farewells.

Pam had been to Amsterdam on a nightmare excursion. She seemed to like the hippy chick boots and incredibly showed no sign of jealousy as I left the Customs Control talking with the Teacher. We went back to Pam's.

All was quite amicable until around bedtime she

accused a spot on my back of being a love bite.

The truth couldn't win over her mindset.

I walked home, ruck sack and all in the pouring rain. Back to England…eh?

Bilge's number was put in my mobile telephone's memory.

I didn't ring her or really think about her.

It was some two or three months later, when Steve Abi and I were travelling back from County versus Sunderland, we spoke again.

We were in the back of Sean Barrow's (another supporter and a solicitor) jeep. The mobile rang. It was Bilge.

She asked me if I remembered her.

"Of course, I replied".

The fact her name came up on the phone's LCD helped recall.

I told her I would ring her on arriving back in Stockport. I explained the background to the lads, all excited.

I rang about eight. She was pleased to talk with me. Bilge was not happy about the family she had been placed with. Chinese.

It strikes me as somewhat lacking in thought that an agency can place a girl who seeks to learn English with a woman who apparently could only speak "pigeon English", so I understand.

The Stadium of Light was brilliant.

We must have spoke again, Bilge and I, but the first date took a while.

I romantically invited her to join me and Steve Abi with Garry Glendenning (Steve's boss) at the County Ground.

Actually home of Swindon Town Football Club.

She was based in Bracknell and so I thought whilst down in these parts give her a call. She agreed, cancelling a prior engagement.

I was amazed.

On the Saturday I borrowed Steve's car and drove to pick her up outside Bracknell Post Office.

I arrived first feeling nervous.

She arrived looking great.

We listened to Turkish tapes travelling west up the M4. Lots of smiling occurred….. a good sign me thought.

We met Steve and Garry in the bar at the Marriott Hotel. She seemed most entertained as we all told Turkish stories and Steve the odd Turkish joke or two. When she got up to powder her face the verdict from the jury was a unanimous "I would".

We drew 1-1 in a drab affair.

I returned her via British Rail and whilst not holding out much hope for further encounters, after all this had hardly been a romantic plan hatched by me, was assured by Steve "you just never know!"

Not a real football fan, but more a basketball type.
Nevertheless, she enjoyed the Swindon experience.

She was dropped off at the station in the Town to
catch the train. I gave her a taxi fare under an
explanation of girls should be careful walking alone late
at night. She was 'fit' but I didn't feel showed any spark
towards me.

On the way home after discussion Steve Abi wisely
said "You just never know what the future will hold for
you two".

I nodded ambivalently.

Bilge did ring to say she had a weekend free and
maybe we could meet up.

We discussed different venues but I surprised her by
picking her up again from the Post Office and driving to
Manchester.

That weekend, we went to Liverpool, meeting up
with Alex Abi (remember, Bilal's distant cousin).

He expressed typical Turkish hospitality by
producing a concocted meal of pizza bits, salad and
more besides.

We made the most of the excursion before returning
to Stockport taking in such sites as the Albert Dock and
Liverpool's Cathedral.

The evening had been pre-arranged with Bilge and I
going out to Efes Taverna via the 'gay village' (a sector
of Manchester where someone has amusingly taken the
'C' off the street sign for Canal Street) with Martin and
Tina.

We met up at Grand Central and Bilge spotted
Martin first.

You see, I had previously described him, as a George

Michael look-a-like.

The atmosphere was relaxed as we sat in the bar and I let slip my first impropriety with a recall of some less than etiquette Turkish phrase "buyuk meme" as a girl passed the window outside.

Literally, big boobs!

This was the only time I'd been a bit rude in front of Bilge - we didn't even hold hands in Merseyside.

It was a memorable evening. Good companionship, food and drink.

The latter an especially fond reminder with Bilge and Tina competing in Tequila slamming stakes.

Martin and I looked on in awe as the Mexican (I think?) liquor went down and down. All this after being told the Restaurant was overbooked for that evening, but they always seemed to find a way of letting me in (remembering me from earlier days with Bilal).

We were the last to leave.

Earlier in the evening, after a girls' trip to the toilets, I was told in confidence "a little birdie informs me she really likes you - but you didn't hear it from me!"

We were to become a relationship.....but for how long?

Bilge was a bit worse for wear...to say the least.

The next day we prepared to return to Bracknell. Bilge informed me that we could only be friends in future rendezvous.

I was saddened but accepted the statement.

I prompted a greater understanding of the reason that we couldn't be more on the return journey, but nevertheless knowing her decision drove to Bracknell and back to Stockport that afternoon and evening.

The next day I rang her.

Then I sent twelve red roses.

Then I threw the last dice with a call to Bilal.

I told him that I was confused. The message passed on by the little bird said she was interested. I was certainly keen.

I simply needed to know was there a chance or should I just get on with my life, alone? He rang her and said something. Then he rang me back and said the news was brilliant …she really liked me but was scared.

She hadn't come to England looking for a boyfriend.

There were plans afoot for that single flat in Istanbul where she would consider options after ceasing to be an au-pair.

Something had started for the second time..thanks Bilal!

I assume that he had convinced her over the phone that "Ady Abi is a good man".

20

We spoke regularly, that is Bilge and I. I ventured down to Berkshire most weekends knowing on passing the Majeski Stadium, home to Reading Football Club - I was nearly there.

I met her friends, who seemed to like me. One Derya described me as "cok tatli" (oh, so sweet!).

Another, named Gul, became a little sister. Her name means a rose. She was short and sweet and accompanied me and Bilge most weekends. One time we all went to Portsmouth to see, Rebecca.

I don't think that I was aware of the real context of au-pairing before.

I met so many Turkish girls all acting as au-pairs.

Every weekend was fun. There was a great trip to Thorpe Park, a theme park off the M25. Approximately, twelve of us went - comprising of three English boys, one married and one in a similar position to me with Turkish counterparts.

The next week we went again to this theme park, with Burcu, Bilge's Cousin, who was sworn to secrecy about the developing relationship.

She was on a two-week exchange to London.

I got the thumbs up from the first family member.

Bilge changed families. No longer was there a China-connection but a nice couple in Winnersh. Apparently the TV Comedian, Lenny Henry, lives here. This couple had a little boy, called Robert.

We started off well. I mean the family and me. An English boyfriend was not a problem. Indeed after my making the effort in politeness, I was invited to stay if I wanted rather than more driving after the Manchester trek.

I discovered the man went to one of my old schools, in Abingdon, and his wife the same, as my sister, Rebecca.

You see after not fulfilling parental aspirations in academia I was transported to a boarding school in my youth.

We always enjoyed each others company.

Bilge and I were very much in love.

In the weeks we talked regularly. The only uncertainty was the future.

Would she return after her two years as an au-pair?

Certainly, I felt if this were the case this was probably a futile relationship as I was getting on. She was in the same deliberation - the song "Should I stay or should I go?" comes to mind.

I didn't exert pressure - what would be would be.

21

Bilge decided to tell her family.

I suspect the brother, Bilen, already knew.

It must have been a nerve-racking experience. After finding out how she broached the subject I was informed that Bilge, with her mother, took the father to see a play "Tore" in a theatre in Izmit (not Izmir!) - the home town. I don't know the story of the play, but it was apparently about a couple that were sought to be separate because of differences in upbringing or something like that.

The family were brought to tears. Bilge then said to her father (in Turkish of course) "What if I fell in love with some one like that?" Baba responded "we would follow your wishes".

Then the introduction to Ady commenced.

Bilge would have made an astute poker player!

Who knows what was actually discussed. I certainly haven't probed. But it was agreed that Bilge could try and find an au-pair job closer to Stockport so that she could have the opportunity to get to know me better and finally decide if this was to be her future.

She returned to England. The following Saturday I arranged for us to have an appointment with the Managing Director of an Au Pair Agency in Stockport. The Agency was recommended by another Turkish girl that was working at the ADA Restaurant.

We were welcomed after encountering the labyrinth of corridors by a diminutive but attractive Helen Morrison, the proprietor.

Within half an hour and after my coincidentally knowing her boyfriend who was introduced (we met in a pub one summer and chatted) all form filling was dispensed with and Bilge appointed to be Helen's personal au-pair in Cheadle Hulme (only a few miles from where I lived).

What a result!

We had many a good time and Bilge settled quickly in to Stockport life.

We still had the romantic endeavours of trips to such as Bolton's Reebok Stadium and Pompey's Fratton Park.

Bilge accepted my regular contact with my Grandma, Marion Stores. She soon loved Grandma and vice versa. Every Sunday was a trip out for Marion and Bilge.

It cannot be easy for a young girl to adapt to an older person being a fixture but my love for my grandmother was not going to disappear.

We started to talk about marriage and I ensured that Grandma despite her age would come to Turkey if a wedding was to ensue.

Christmas 1998 was a typical homely affair with just Grandma and I, at 'Manisa'.

We spent an entire week together at my house and loved it all.

Bilge telephoned from Turkey and Bilal sent a mobile telephone text message "Cok tesekkurler, we love you. Happy new year. Never forget you Abi".

Grandma passed away in Stepping Hill Hospital early in January, leaving one woman in my life.

I had been telephoned earlier in the morning by the Warden at her sheltered accommodation.

I was informed that there was no answer on the obligatory morning check of her flat. A carpenter was being called to prise open the door.

I couldn't wait and sped to the accommodation in

Edgeley - just up from County's ground.

I kicked in the door and found Grandma unconscious initially, then a few words, then comatosed. The ambulance operators came and carted her off.

I spent circa. 20 hours by her bedside some with Bilge and later my Dad and Rebecca who had caught the train up from Oxford.

I left for just two hours as West Bromwich Albion was unmoved, seeking a consultancy report by facsimile transfer the same night.

She died after exhausted breathing around 4.00am. I broke the news to all on my return home.

I planned the execution of the funeral, which went okay. I even visited the Chapel of Rest beforehand which surprised me.

The burial went okay though the undertakers were clearly from a Carry On Movie. My Armani jacket was stolen from the accompanying hearse whilst the church ceremony by a slightly feminine, red-faced clergyman conducted the proceedings.

Bilge was in attendance supporting me all the way… so was Steve Abi and my Accountants.

I delivered my final speech to Grandma:

"Marion Stores

I could not let today go without saying a few words about Marion Stores, known to me as Grandma, but really she was a lot more to me than this title would suggest.

She never had an easy life, spending her working life as a cleaner.

Her husband, Bill was not the easiest of people.

She has always been a Stockport resident. I knew her initially from Hollywood but latterly Edgeley. Bill, that's Grandad, and Grandma lived in Edgeley at two homes on Old Chapel Street and then at St Lesmo Road.

They never owned their own home.

My parents gave birth to me whilst still at Manchester University studying to be doctors. Thus, for around the first four years of my life Grandma brought me up. It was because of these early years that I believe the psychological bonding began.

I remember vividly many life events fondly of this additional mother in my life.

I was very fortunate indeed to have had the pleasure of knowing Marion Stores. "

Grandma was a devoted wife. To her dying day she attended regularly the grave of Grandad, and where she will later be laid to rest, tidying the plot and planting flowers. I will be left to continue the tradition and shall do so whilst I remain capable.

I feel that like many elderly people, she would have died soon after Grandad in 1994 if I hadn't been there for her. I don't seek praise for this statement as it was a partnership.

We supported each other.

My girlfriend at the time Sue and I took her to Scotland for a break after Grandad passed away. She thoroughly enjoyed the experience. Later Pam my next girlfriend invited her to spend Christmas Day 1997 with her parents in Leigh. She was given the black and white fluffy cat you may have seen on the coffin today. After several visits to Grandma's flat at my request she gave it a name and called him Timothias. Never a day went by without her talking to the cat. She was fond of such toys and the family members will cherish the numerous crotchet dolls she talently made. I have three characters: a father and son in Stockport County replica kits and a small doll.

Grandma was very independent and coped at the ripe old age of 87 with walks up to Castle Street for shopping and her pension. During the last few months I made her meals and know like the back of my hand her preferences. Like her father before, she was a Stockport County fan. How many people do you know at 86 years old have gone to Edgeley Park to support the local team. In recent years she has started to forget somethings but she'd always be able to tell you the County score on a Saturday evening.

She combined her love of fluffy characters and County by adoring the current mascot, Vernon Bear. This character is actually one of my friends and regularly she asked me "how's the bear".

Just two weeks ago it was agreed that she would soon start to receive visits from Social Services. She made me laugh as she said she was going to "dodge" them by either going out or not answering the door.

Grandma changed in the last four years. Initially after Grandad's bereavement she was warm from a distance. The kiss on my cheek on my departure from her house later became a warm embrace and kiss on the lips.

I never forget after my housing a professional Turkish footballer at my home and how she held out her arms wide and cuddled Bilal like her very own family on his announcing that he would be returning to his own Country. I have already had condolences from three people in Turkey since news of her death. This says it all about the appeal of this woman.

I don't have too many regrets. A minimum of three days a week have been spent together in the last few years. At Christmas she stayed with me for a week. On the night before the tragedy I took chips and steak and kidney pudding round and we ate together and watched television. Then she walked to the front door and waved me goodbye as I drove off. This became part of our ritual.

I was alerted to the fact that she wasn't answering the door last Wednesday. I kicked her door down and found her semi-concious on her bed. She asked me "what day is it". We went to Stepping Hill hospital and I talked to her continually whilst she lay comatosed in Casualty, then Emergency Admissions Unit and finally in Ward B2. The doctors said they weren't sure she could hear me. Bilge and Rebecca spoke to her also. I knew she could hear and wouldn't give in. She arrived with a diagnosis of possible stroke, heart attack, hypothermia or diabetic crisis. Her blood pressure was abnormal also. Within the last hour of her life she had fought all symptoms. For example, her blood sugar with the aid of intravenous insulin had reduced from the 'sky high' 30 on admission to a much more acceptable 17. I believe she tried everything in her powers to live, to her credit. The 'killer' would have been the kidneys which we couldn't get to restart, though pneumonia and the lungs brought the inevitable to a speedy conclusion.

We did have a final communication. She calmed down when I told her that she'd had a little fall and was now in hospital to try and get better. Her minimal conversation included "I love you" in response to my same expression to her. She stopped breathing, I hope without too much internal pain.

I had to see her just one more time. In the chapel of rest I have laid favourite momentoes to remain with her. All I can say is that within this coffin "she looks beautiful, dressed in a silk gown with veil".

Grandma will never be forgotten. I've already seen her in Stockport and my dreams.

I still see Grandad under many a flat cap in the Streets. This is the true meaning of love.

Last year my office was named Marion Stores House as anyone walking Stockport Road, Cheadle will see engraved in the front of the building. She said to me on many an occasion that she doesn't know what she'd have done without me. Equally, I couldn't have done without her.

Marion Stores will be a large loss in my life and Stockport.

Grandma rest in peace and remember that I will always be here for you!

Bilge told her Dad about my bereavement.

He kindly passed on his sympathies. I had not met him, nor spoken with him. The concept of possibly settling down with his daughter, I felt, would mean I was not really flavour of the moment.

I'd seen his photograph and know he was something like former President of the Teacher's Union in Turkey.

It was a challenge that I would need to face if going to continue with Bilge.

I spoke to Suat at the ADA Restaurant one night and he said you will go through a ritual….if this is to result. I remember thinking of the key points in assessing my chances of pulling this off.

(1) NOT A MUSLIM;

(2) OLDER and

(3) ENGLISH.

Now how does that sound in evaluating the probability of a win.

This was clearly going to be a real six-pointer!

We decided to get engaged and this was going to be done properly.

In Turkey, it is not the man who normally asks for the woman's hand in marriage, but the respective parents that will seek permission.

Olga, my mum and Clive, my step-dad would accompany me. Greg, my real dad would send a letter (that I duly scribed) together with photographs.

We were met in August Nineteen Ninety-Nine at Adnan Menderes (the airport) by Bilge's dad,

"Baba".

He transported the four of us to Ayvalik, not Izmit.

You see in the summer they were one of many families that migrated from the industrial employment areas to more pleasant environs. The family had a holiday home in this resort, in a suburb of Ayvalik called "Saramsakli" - that means 'with garlic'.

We stopped once on the way at Baba Anne's apartment (Bilge's Grandma on her dad's side in a place called Aliaga). We were welcomed with open arms and warm hearts.

The conversation was somewhat restricted but "yumurtali ekmek ve peynir" (eggy bread and nice feta-like cheese) together with other accompaniments made for a hearty breakfast.

The Grandma and I shared smiles throughout. Hospitality was second to none and not a hint of antagonism.

Later we went on to Ayvalik where we were met by Anne, Bilge's mum, Bilen kardes and an array of aunts, uncles and a few younger relatives.

Shoes are taken off as a matter of courtesy - a custom that I was already familiar with from previous trips.

The proposed in-laws were pleasant and tried to welcome us in every way.

The dad was initially warmer and the brother and I soon bonded.

Okay reference to the latest football gossip surrounding the Turkish League broke the ice, but have I said before football is an International language.

They were a family of Galatasaray supporters.

I was soon taught the chorus of "Cim Bom Bom" - the call of the fanatical fans reflecting the Cim Bom Stadyum.

We stayed in a local hotel sorted out by the deposit

of some American Dollars by Baba. As my parents prepared for a nap, I walked around the market.

Rebecca caught me on the mobile to let me know that Greg had become a Professor at Oxford University. I hadn't even known it was in the offing but was nevertheless delighted for him.

Then I heard a beep from a car horn to discover the entire future family traversing behind. I leapt in the car with a gesture to board and drove to a car space before shopping for fruit, vegetables and ladies jeans.

I passed on the news about my dad's appointment and Bilge translated her dad's congratulations on my father's appointment.

University of Oxford is a universal brand too.

I sensed that they wanted the formalities addressed quick.

We discussed the ensuing probability of engagement around a terrific barbecue in the back yard.

Both mothers were forced to tears - and I felt similar as I was advertised as such a wonderful product.

Raki, the traditional drink, sure made the evening go smoothly with any frigidity broken down and much frivolity and laughter.

The next night was more formal.

Just Bilge and parents and me.

I was questioned about career, worth, intentions and politics - and the fact that my Grandad was a "buyuk socialist" certainly went down well.

As to the latter I did not respond but simply repeated a well-versed home truth taught to me in my childhood by Grandad - "never discuss politics or religion". Bill Stores spoke some sense.

I was accepted.

Then the "couple to be" and Bilen went to the Centre

94

of Ayvalik to purchase engagement rings.

I felt shattered as we visited one jewellery shop after another. It wasn't assisted by my lack of control over the decision-making.

I wanted to buy Bilge the diamond that she deserved and was constantly faced with the "brilliant stone" (so the dictionary translated) that the sales men offered.

I hadn't heard of this jewel alternative and convinced my self that this held all the potential of a typical naive tourist's rip-off scenario.

I tried to telephone an acquaintance in Kusadasi who had his own jewellery shop to discover the truth. My mobile wasn't operative in Turkey and the PTT had no listing of my friend by Surname or Shop Name. The dissimilarities with the efficiency of 192 in my homeland served to wind me up more and more.

It took "Lahmacun" (local pizza) and "Ayran" (milky drink) for the first time to revert me to calm.

Eventually we opted for a gorgeous diamond ring, which I duly paid for with Mastercard.

We returned to Saramsakli by dolmus and were met by Baba.

He took us immediately to another jeweller and purchased for me a unique gold ring with white gold insert running central throughout. Also, a nice gold bracelet which whilst not my usual attire, nevertheless was a gesture that was much appreciated.

The evening comprised of the traditional Turkish engagement ceremony conducted by Bilge's big uncle.

I had drank much Raki though by accident Anne (Bilge's mum) seemed to quaff mine also.

The celebration resulted in the tying of rings with a red ribbon and an officiating cut. Strips of ribbon were then given out to selected members of the audience.

A final cake cutting concluded the formal event.

It was sad to see both Anne and Baba crying at a joyous occasion.

But this was considered to be a big sacrifice, of that I had no doubt.

Yet not as big a commitment as Bilge was making in accepting an invitation to be my wife in England.

The younger ones then all departed to a local bar.

It was outside in a garden with much greenery and trees. Live Turkish music was played all night and all the people danced and sang with intervals of waving lit sparklers.

Even I danced after all it was my engagement party.

I'm sure the relatives soon realised that Bilge wasn't marrying me for my nifty footwork.

I've never experienced such an atmosphere in an English bar.

Alcohol was an extra ingredient, not necessary for the fun.

This was total enjoyment as the youth of Turkey enjoyed their pride in being within this Republic.

We left for a walk to the seafront and to taste the Ayvalik Toastie.

I got slightly jealous by an old, male friend monopolising Bilge's conversations.

Bilen noticed and told off his sister.

23

We met Baba's brothers and families.

Baba was the middle one in age. Big brother ran a construction business building villas, Little brother was a GP in Aliaga. Both brothers were great in different ways but the builder had the most repetitive sense of humour.

He reminded me of my Uncle David in Canada - often described as the "black sheep" in our family - but one with which I had great empathy.

Bilge's uncles had both married sisters.

We visited Seytan Sofrasi - the fictional, footprint of the devil in its eroded stone location in the hills above Ayvalik. It was a far better version of the Wizzard at Alderley Edge in Cheshire.

The Turks had realised the potential and introduced such necessities of commercialism as bars and catering.

The view across the surrounding seas and islands was incredible with astonishing beauty.

Never had I experienced such attractiveness in my previous trips to this Country.

We went on several nights out - all people from England and Turkey - to sample the delicacies of Turkish foods. This paragraph remains short as it's far too mouth watering to recounter the way in which my taste buds were so treated.

One particular memory was the trip we took on the boat around Cunda (pronounced Junder) Island. Sun, sea and copious amounts of fish (like whitebait), fresh salads and beer or raki. I dived off the boat with others - it must have housed around 150 passengers that day. I swam with the family, ate with them, joked and laughed - without too much talk. I taught Bilen a trick; you know when you place pebbles on the underside of the elbow face up, rotate the wrist and rapidly flick your arm down to catch them before they fall. Simple things met with growing warmth.

I had certainly been adopted as "damat" as big uncle kept reminding me.

Damat is son-in-law.

We returned to the Airport a week later. I had after several attempts managed to contact Bilal and he said that he would try and make it to see me before my departure. I thought it unlikely with his commitment, necessarily so, to the football season - he was still at Aydin Spor.

You see we were departing around 3.00am.

Bilge and her father hang around a while but Bilal didn't appear.

At least not until they gave up the ghost - he suddenly arrived with Meltem and Metin.

We only got around fifteen minutes together but I shared photographs of the engagement event and we drank and shared fond memories.

It was good to see them all, especially Bilal.

24

The wedding was set for Friday 5th November
Nineteen Ninety Nine (the English one that is)!
Bonfire night.

After the usual protestations with the Authorities we
secured visas for Bilge's mum, dad and brother.

They arrived a week before the wedding. I enjoyed
their company as they stayed in our new house. They
brought several hand made furnishings which
brightened up the home. We went to Warwick Castle
(shut early), Alton Towers (closed) and the Wizzard in
Alderley Edge near to the home of the Beckham family.

I didn't realise that the winter really is a closed
season for tourists.

Bilge's parents woke first every morning. They
always strolled down to Cheadle's shops and bought the
English equivalent of "borek" which we ate for
breakfast every day - like a real family.

The words that were repeated most were "deprem".

Turkey and in fact Bilge's home town of Izmit
suffered a horrendous earthquake back in September.
This was the topic of everyone's conversation.

The family and relatives survived but there were
several acquaintances and pupils who died from Bilge's
father's and mother's schools. The pictures that we saw
on Sky Digital everyday were moving and tragic. Often
Bilge was moved to tears.

I even tried via Steve Abi to organise a fundraiser - a
match between Stockport County and Yallova
(apparently their stadium was being used as a settling
ground for stretchers and the injured after the
earthquake). But we couldn't trace the officials from
that Club.

Bilge and I travelled to watch Turkey play Northern Ireland in the Euro 2000 qualifiers. The Irish commenced proceedings by translating in to Turkish the fond wishes and regrets to the people of Turkey about the recent quake.

The Turkish contingent responded by outsinging the Province's home fans throughout the game with the repetitive song of "Northern Ireland".

Turkey appreciated the gesture! We, they ..Turkey, won 3-0 and I collected all the players' autographs one by one at the Airport for Bilge's little brother.

The Wedding day neared and Bilen and I said our obligatory farewells as we headed off to the Waterside Hotel in Didsbury for a day in quarantine.

We wished to oblige the traditional custom of not spending time with the bride the day before the ceremony.

My adopted brother, Bilen (he was my appointed best man) and I swam, ate and drank. At least I drank alcohol as my nerves were getting the better of me.

The Wedding ran well. Traditional November weather meant that it rained on the day but this was more than offset by the warmth of the English and Turkish guests mingling with one another.

Bilge looked radiant.

I remembered the advice from one friend, a girl, to tell my wife to be how beautiful she looked as she traversed down the aisle in Cheadle Village's church.

Apparently on her wedding day the groom started his commentary by saying "you won't believe what I scored on the golf course this morning".

I even looked slim (well slimmer....weight loss attributable to stress).

The video of the day shall be cherished forever more

(and was so much more professional than my earlier production which was attempting to promote the Onat Hotel).

The speeches were funny, even the Onat video was reproduced with humorous dubbing of both Bilal and myself, courtesy of Martin.

Turkish music was in abundance and raki quaffed.

For purposes of creating the atmosphere I recollect my speech:

I've told the tale many a time of how I came back from Turkey three years ago.

Most travellers to this Country return with rugs, jewellery and leather. I returned with a professional Turkish footballer, Bilal - and tried to secure him a contract to play in England, but to no avail.

It would have taken something out of the ordinary to beat this story - well now I've done it.

It's probably the basis of a Mills and Boon, romantic novel - but I met Bilge on 4th January 1998 on a plane journey back from Istanbul. I sat next to her. Neither of us could really speak in one another's languages and so we communicated via finger pointing to the respective sections of our Turkish-English, English-Turkish dictionaries.

This was to become the start of our relationship, which has culminated in our wedding today.

We still humour each other by referring to this destiny by an affectionate quote of

"Cok Tesekkur Ederim Turk Hava Yollari"

- for those of you not fluent in the Turkish language that is

"Thank you Turkish Airlines".

I've grown to love Turkey since originally being

introduced by Steve Bellis. I remember saying to him at the time that I don't understand people who keep going back to the same destination rather than trying out holidays in different resorts around the World. That was some fourteen trips ago. I am now fortunate enough to have this as my second home with this matrimonial tie today.

I have to thank my parents and stepparents for getting me to where I am in my life today. Greg my Dad and stepmother, Christina. Olga, my Mother, and stepfather Clive. And I am fortunate enough to now have another mum and dad in Bilge's parents - Anne and Baba. They have been wonderful in accepting me in to their family.

Despite the differences in language and culture they have made me most welcome.

"Hos geldiniz and Tesekkur Ederim."

My only sadness is that my remaining parents in this quartet, my grandparents - Bill and Marion are not here for this occasion. At least Grandma met Bilge for which I am pleased. Indeed, Bilge sat with me whilst Grandma, passed away at Stepping Hill Hospital earlier this year.

A traumatic experience in joining a family to be - but she coped admirably and this says much about the character and caring nature of my wife.

I also have a remarkable sister in Rebecca - but I can't wait until she drops the baby to get back to her renown drinking form.

And now I have a brother, my best man today, Bilen - Bilge's little brother, kardes.

I am delighted to have so many of our friends in the room today. For purposes of introduction these include my relatives, friends from School, friends from College and friends from Stockport and its hinterland. I'm not referring to you all in this speech but the mere fact that you are hear today shows how much you mean to us. I would like to mention at this stage: Nikki and Graham - good friends in work and play; Alwin and Shirley - a couple who have welcomed us regularly and help me immensely in my career; Alex and Tracey - from Birkenhead - Alex is from Bilal's home village of Yenikoy - you remember Bilal was the footballer who lived with me and feels part of my real family; Mark and Rachel - former colleagues and friends and Suat and Gillian another great Turkish friend who resides in Stockport.

I'm sure that you will agree that the bridesmaids look adorable. Can I introduce: Tina (a friend for Bilge and myself for life), Gul, Derua and Helen plus the little ones Holly, Abi, Chloe and pageboy James.

As for the ushers - what a motley crew. But nevertheless, the true meaning of mates for which I am especially pleased to have such good friends. Simon Bishop, my best buddy from School with whom I've shared many a good time. Steve Bellis, the person who is responsible for introducing me to all my close friends in Stockport. And of course, Bilen, my recently adopted brother. Then there is Martin Bellis - who has helped me admirably in today's preparations, Spud (who has probably done more for me and my past grandparents than anyone), Big John - who's having his own Turkish rendezvous at the moment, Mark "Furry" Furness my good pal from Sheffield University - sat there with his lovely wife Vicky, Steve Salmon from Portsmouth Polytechnic, Simon Dawson and Jamie. I'm sure we will continue to have many a good laugh in years to come - both Bilge and me with such wonderful people.

103

I'm supposed to say a few words about my darling Bilge.

"Askim. Seni cok seviyorum". I love you so much.

I feel that I am a very lucky person to have the privilege of being accepted as your husband. I hope that I can do justice to the sort of life that she deserves.

Bilge is the most wonderful girl that I have ever met. Not only does she have a brilliant personality - but she's also gorgeous. She modestly refers to herself in her well-versed English as "I am bloody marvellous".

Learning the most important things first in her native tongue, I have learnt to sing the chorus of "I'm horny, horny, horny" - in Turkish, but it probably wouldn't be respectful to recite this just now. Thanks must go to Martin for teaching her an array of colloquial phrases at our first official date when Tina, Martin, Bilge and I went to Efes Taverna, a Turkish Restaurant in Manchester, for a night never to be forgot. The events that were to unfold and the start of our relationship are the most memorable, but I won't forget in a hurry Tina and Bilge challenging each other to a Tequila Slammer drinking competition.

Bilge's practical application of the English language has left a few more memories with me. I can't make too much fun being incompetent at her own Country's language - something that I must improve upon. Though Big John has offered to go to College with me to tackle this subject.

The two stories I will tell are clean ones that tickle me!

Once in London whilst sat in a park in one of our earlier romantic encounters we cuddled closely and she looked in my eyes and said "Oh Adrian you're so huge!"

I can't forget this and said "Thanks, darling".

Apparently she got the words "huge" and "cute" confused but the impression was left.

The second example relates to a bet that she and I had relating to a recent movie.

She was adamant that Julia Roberts latest film at the Cinema with Hugh Grant was called "Stepping Hill". Infact this is the name of our local Hospital in Stockport and it was indeed "Notting Hill" that she was looking for.

To date we haven't had a serious argument. Long may it continue. I play a little game at times of minor disagreement. We simply look in to each other's eyes and I say if I can count to ten and you don't give me a big smile or laugh then this is a serious argument. Each time so far she ends up falling about laughing so it seems a good psychological method for diffusing a situation.

Bilge has had an amazing impact on Turkey-England relations. She is loved by all my friends.

This impact is reflected by Spud in a trip in September to Northern Ireland. He commented that he couldn't get too excited about a Country other than his own. These were the comments from a lad who travelled to Belfast for the weekend to watch Turkey play in the European Championships and spent the full 90 minutes dancing and singing with the Turkey contingent. It was amazing how well the lyrics conjured up by Big John of "We don't know the words"

seemed to fit so perfectly with all the songs sung by the supporters that afternoon.

Today is a very special day for me - and I thank you all for being here and sharing it with Bilge and myself.

Please enjoy the proceedings and sit back to hear

firstly- a few words from my Dad who has recently been awarded a professorship at Oxford University in recognition for his medical achievements especially with children - a noteworthy first, a brave speech from Bilen, the best man who is attempting a presentation in a language foreign to him; and subsequently Simon Bishop- friendship since school days, Steve Bellis representing Stockport friends; Mark Furness - companionship starting at University; and Martin Bellis.

And finally please join me in a toast to my wife, Bilge and our Turkish friends.

A wonderful day was had by all. Especially my wife and I.

Extra Time

25

We didn't return to Turkey until 7th February 2000.

We had wanted to go for the Millennium but Bilge's passport hadn't been returned, post-marriage, in time.

Anyway we returned.

This was the first time I'd gone to their home town of Izmit.

It was the first time that Bilge had gone back since the earthquake.

Buildings were adorned with "stretch marks" and a myriad of the population remained under canvas in makeshift accommodation.

It was saddening.

I saw people doing their best to continue with lives. A pharmacy still traded without any shop frontage. Night time brought the erection of a cage of metal bars......but I felt a devious tyrant in the United Kingdom would still steal the drugs on display. Only a fishing rod would be necessary to catch the contents on the still visible shelving through this makeshift security measure.

I learnt all about the family's upbringing and toured various destinations in the Town.

One night we got an aftershock.

The seismology department at either Ankara or Istanbul showed it up to be 4.2 on its web page.

I pretended that I thought it to be a passing lorry to inject humour in to the event. Really I knew what it was and suffered my first panic attack in response.

It can't be appreciated just what it must be like to live under this constant fear of a repeat of this disaster. So many of the buildings are high rise and a strike from the earth's core would leave no exit route.

I only slept sporadically with the self induced fear of another strike.

We met all the family - especially on Bilge's mum side this time. They all made me most welcome and I feel liked me.

We trekked to Sapanca, a supposedly beautiful lake, but on arrival discovered the lake had burst from its containment - another symptom from the earthquake. What had been a resort was now no more than a war zone. Destroyed and under water with little hope for recovery. We headed up to the hills and ate 'mantar' (mushroomy raviolli-like pasta parcels) and drank cay. The whole family, that was. Then sat within a log cabin at the foot of a scenic waterfall.

We had visited for the view but also to catch our own fresh water fish for supper from a designated fish farm.

A beetle strolled across the window (in this cay ev) and I was informed that if I touched it I would smell something. It was of the farting insect variety apparently.

I quipped "does the same thing happen if I touch the fish".

They laughed at this token joke.

Later, a day trip took us to Silivri on the outskirts of Istanbul. We passed Atakoy and I remembered the area as we drove passed.

It was where I deboarded the bus from the Airport to stay at Hotel Inter in Beyazit. I wondered if, Metin the Steward was still there, no doubt, if so, "as pissed as an elephant".

Amazing how somethings come back to you at times.

All the family relatives welcomed us as returning heroes and despite the language barrier I always felt at home.

We booked the Klassis Hotel in Silivri for the second half of our wedding plans. It was executive-like and at a price far more competitive than an English counterpart. Anyway, a popular choice and accessible.

Before being dropped off in Istanbul for a night with Bilge's ex-University friends we ate at Bilge's mother's little brother's house and I watched "Telly Tubbies" on TV. Not my favourite programme but I remember looking at the home of Poh, Lala and whoever and thinking it reminded me of so many of the canvas structures the poor natives were presently taking to be their homes following the 'deprem' in Izmit.

Istanbul was really discovered for the first time that night.

We had a fantastic night with live musicians in a restaurant in Taksim.

We stayed at Aycan's, a home mate from University in Ankara. And the next day, breakfast was a Pinar Burger and cok cay at another Teahouse bordering the sea. We sat for an hour or two under Mehmet Sultan Bridge and I thought.....I could really live here.

Before returning to England, I took in a trip to Kocaelispor. The home football team of Izmit, languishing in the bottom half of the Turkish Premier division.

Rather than recite my opinions on the game I illustrate the event with my write up that Steve Abi asked me to prepare in a Match Day magazine for Stockport County on my return.

Kocaelispor

Stockport County has been known to have links to the Country of Turkey. Marketing Manager, Steve Bellis has previously worked in the resort of Kusadasi on the Aegean coast. Club Secretary, Gary Glendenning, former Captain Andy Thorpe, and Assistant Marketing Manager, Chris Jolley have taken vacations - to name but a few. Vernon Bear also!

Rumour has it that Carlo Nash has been seen strutting his stuff in a Turkish Restaurant in Stockport.

And we won't go in to Stadium Manager, Bish's experience over there?

From next season, we will be featuring regular updates on one Turkish team, Kocaelispor (pronounced Cojellyspor)

in County's Match Day Magazine, courtesy of native resident, Bilen Kur and Cheadle's Acrobat Consulting & Marketing (our marketing and fundraising consultants).

The team presently languishing in the wrong half of the Turkish Premier Division has similarities to us. They are to be found in the shadows of the larger clubs in Istanbul such as Galatasaray, Fenerbache and Besiktas.

The bigger name signings are often cast offs from Istanbul's elite and Trabzon Spor.

In keeping with the ethos of Stockport County as "the friendly football club" - we have adopted this team for the next campaign.

The Club is located at the epicentre of the tragic earthquake in Turkey in the last quarter of 1999.

Whilst County supporters were returning from Loftus Road (Q.P.R), Adrian Stores, Managing Director at Acrobat was watching Kocaelispor versus Erzurum

(City in the East of the Country) at our adopted team's home stadium in Izmit on the outskirts of Istanbul.

The team hadn't played at home since the earthquake. Erzurum's players made a nice gesture by parading the pitch pre-kick off with a banner announcing that they were sorry to learn about the tremors and substantial damage done to Kocaelispor's town.

It was not posted as a big game with both teams at the foot of the Division. Hence, an extortionate 75 pence was the admission fee for an adult.

An estimated 15,000 turned up nevertheless.

Kocaelispor had played most of its games away from home because of the earthquake. The game with Erzurum was one that must be won to redress the poor league position. They got the ideal start with a headed goal at the far post from Russian, Kamoltzen (Kamo, for short) and increased the lead on 31 minutes after a tricky bit of skill and shot from twenty yards by winger, Serdar.

The Referee showed no sympathy to the home side and the terraces roared with jingles, which questioned his sexual preferences.

Some football songs appear of a universal nature!

Serdar was booked for dissent before Mirko made it three nil before half time. The winger's hand of god mirroring Maradona's exploits left him not merely looking red faced as the second card was shown to him on 53 minutes. Ten men, Kocaeli completed the rout through Dabro on 71. 4 - 0 was how it finished despite the crowd's crying for "bes" ("we want five").

The team left to a rapturous applause and the atmosphere was electric.

The victory had gone a small way to taking the

locals minds off the recent events. The result leaves Kocaelispor in 16th out of 18 with Erzurum two points the better, on 22, in 14th place. Galatasaray tops the table with 48 points and a game in hand over second placed Besiktas (eight points behind) and then Fenerbache.

Of possible interest to today's supporters includes Besiktas star player is Amokachi - the Nigerian striker formerly of Everton; Gordon Milne - ex Leicester City Boss managed Fenerbache to a serious of successes; and Galatasaray's (GS) former Manager was Graeme Souness who seems mainly remembered for planting the 'GS' flag in the centre circle after winning the Cup Final against Fenerbache (arch rivals).

More news from Turkey before long…………

ADRIAN STORES

It was a similar experience to when my Grandad took me to Edgeley Park for the first taste of football. An experience that made me a supporter of that Club (Stockport County).

Bilen and Bilge's father took me. The latter bought me a Kocaelispor hat, which I needed on that very cold evening. We got victory (I say we as this team had become mine on that continent).

I noticed that all Turkish teams have an 'Amigo'.

He conjures up the atmosphere by remonstrating with the fans in the ground to get behind their team. Vocally that is....

Images of the game in Belfast were rekindled. The first time that I had experienced an Amigo at a football match.

We left 5 minutes before the end to avoid the rush.

The gates were not opened for some reason and I started to fear a repeat of Hillsbrough

- Baba, Bilen and I squashed against the outpour of supporters at the final whistle.

I searched frantically for any crevice in to which we could squeeze to save our lives. The inevitable didn't result... thankfully... as the fans seemed to respond with common sense and avoid prolonging the rush and bedlam.

26

The Wedding in Turkey came around soon, on 15th April 2000.

Unlike the English event (which I managed) Bilge's parents dealt admirably with the organisation. They even selected an invitation, which came with a BA embossed in a heart on the card.

Now where had I experienced these initials before?

English companions visited with me. My mum and I travelled from Manchester with Turkish Airlines. Spud, Martin and Tina came via London with BA! Sarah and Bethan were two girls who also travelled from down South to enjoy the festivities.

The male contingent of the Kur family met us at the Airport on arrival….and Bilge, of course.

We were unaware just what sort of venue we would initially be booked in to.

The Hotel, Arcadia in Sultan Ahmed, Istanbul was the choice.

It had been arranged via the fiancé of one of Bilge's University friends. He was its Manager.

What a choice? Arcadia was superb. We met the others from England on its roof terrace, in the bar, on the eighth floor. Arguably, it had one of the best views within Istanbul. It faced, the famous landmark of the Blue Mosque, alternatively known as Sultan Ahmet Mosque. It reminded me, at night all lit up, of the fantasy palace that is shown as a magical destiny before or after Disney movies.

Bilal wouldn't be at the wedding.

He couldn't be released from his present team, then Turgutlu Spor. Somewhere near Manisa surprise, surprise.

No doubt another prison?

Nevertheless, he, Meltem, Apo and Oner sent fond regards and best wishes.

Can you believe the second B still hadn't met the first B despite several conversations.

The first night in the Country, before the Wedding, we travelled in to Taksim to enjoy live music and copious Efes Pilsen.

For the first time I felt a little nervy - this merely a week after the Galatasaray debacle. The atmosphere in a quaint underground bar was warm and much fun had by all. I had become a 'sort of Turk' by adoption by Bilge's family, but would the outside world realise this - or see 'England' stamped on my forehead?

Anyway, we mixed with Turks on adjoining tables and the lead vocalist congratulated Bilge and I on the forthcoming ceremony.

Bilge left the next morning early with Tina and my mum for the ritual hairdressing. It lasted some four hours! I sat for the last hour waiting outside for a first viewing with eager anticipation.

We arrived some 50 minutes before kick off.

I dressed speedily in a suit, made by UKI, bought by Baba and Anne, as is tradition. Bilge wore the same dress as in England and was simply stunning.

I had a few drinks to keep calm with Tina who had become Bilge's best friend in England and helped with the ritual dressing.

We awaited the call to come to the function room. We exited the lift on ground floor level to be met by three of Bilge's friends (now mine also) who paparazzi like took pictures of the Bride and Bride and Groom.

They were Ebru, Aycan and Bihim.

We were then notified that National TV Station,

Show, were present for filming.

We entered the room to rapturous applause.

It was like make-believe.

High ceilings, silk table clothes and gold decorations covering each chair.

Bilge and I, like Becks and Posh, had a special table for two up front.

I recall I was somewhat like Zebedee.

Constantly, springing up and down from the seating as one after another the Turks came to congratulate the couple, placing gold bracelets by abundance on Bilge's wrist and pinning gold sovereigns of Ottoman origin to us both. We also received a $20 note and Bilge a ring.

We felt like royalty.

I simply said "tesekkur ederim and memnun oldum" (thank you and nice to meet you to all as they kissed me and passed by).

The bouncing meant that not much food was eaten by me or my wife.

It looked great but it was only the alcohol that I had time for.

Live music was played and the Turkish guests rose and danced majestically to the array of music.

The English joined in on some and despite my inability to click my fingers, I enjoyed the experience.

But I didn't half sweat! I wore a waistcoat and yellow cravat beneath the dark grey suit.

Baba gave a short speech. I have no idea what was said but his mobile rang mid-way through which tickled the audience.

There was one dance that Baba instigated. It was one I hadn't seen before back home at such restaurants as Efes Taverna, Amphora or ADA.

It was impressive.

The three men and later two women taking part swooped like eagles majestically in some kind of traditional movement.

Everyone was filmed throughout by amateur, Bilen and Show TV.

Towards the end we were whisked off to one side of the room for a question and answer interview by the television crew.

I had mentally prepared. I was not surprised by the focus on Galatasaray and Leeds United in the repertoire.

Bilge was asked to translate each question and my response. Politician like, I ducked and dived and remained focussed on the festivity as a joyous occasion. I simply said that things should not be taken out of context and in my opinion after viewing footage in both countries - both sets of hooligans were to blame. There is an element of instigators or hooligans in all countries in the World.

I had experienced same in Italy at an England versus Rome encounter some years back.

I mentioned that the loss of two lives was unacceptable in what is after all simply sport.

The media did a terrific job of accentuating the difficulties.

Reporting in England was biased.

In Turkey it showed English, not Leeds necessarily, fighting in the South of France in the last Euro championships - focussing constantly on one Stockport County yob burning a flag. I understand that the individual concerned had been banned for life from Edgeley Park.

Asked who I supported I said "Kocaelispor!"

Now that threw them!

119

Apparently I scored well in the "post-match" ratings.

The morning after Bilge and I swam in the best pool I have known. Bath water-hot in temperature and access so we could swim straight through from the indoor to the outdoor pool - where it seemed even hotter.

We visited Anne Anne's traditional house in Fenerköy (literally, Torch Village).

It reminded me of Oner's mum's residence in Yeniköy.

We had certainly become a family.

Friendship beyond frontiers.

I loved them all, and they, I felt, me.

Returning to Arcadia, we arranged various tours.

We visited the Blue Mosque.

Spud had to pull up his Stockport County socks to his shorts to comply with the covering of the naked flesh criteria. The facility was fantastic.

One man stopped us all in the streets of Istanbul to say that he was saddened by the recent clash with Leeds United in the City.

A most sincere gesture and one echoed throughout the trip.

We then came to Yerebatan Cistern, the flooded palace. A venue beneath the ground with origins dating back to the fifth century.

The Grand Bazaar completed the tour.

That night we ate traditional Turkish food - my mum sloped off to kindly pay the bill for the remaining English contingent.

Then Bihim, Aycan and Bilge took Spud, Martin and I to smoke the spirit water. It was traditional, non-drug, pastime - with bongs containing chocolate and fruit cocktail!

A very different experience. The owner didn't quite see the funny side of Spud blowing, rather than the intended sucking of, the water-filled pipe!

All of us had a great and memorable time over only four days.

Bilal still hadn't met Bilge.

We had to now return to the Au Pair Agency in England, that Bilge and I bought off Helen Morrison - and I was due to start a GCSE in Turkish in Manchester this autumn.

Show TV and other channels would be installed in our Stockport home and I would await a life of regular friendly encounters between friends at home, away and in totally different cultures ...... where something just gelled!

Golden Goal

27

Incredibly, it wasn't until the summer of 2002, in August, that B met B.

There had been many occasions that had promised Bilal meeting Bilge.

But none had come to fruition.

We had remained in touch largely via SMS messaging, but on a slightly less regular basis.

Bilal, now at Buca Spor in the second division had a friendly match in the afternoon and would be in Ayvalik to see me by 10.00pm.

He caught the autobus and Baba took me to pick him up with Bilen. We met at a bus stop outside the house of a former goalkeeper to the National team and Galatasaray - a guy called Hayrettin.

Love is strong.

It was just like we'd never been apart.

This is the case with true friends when long absences do not reduce affections.

Bilal did admit to worrying slightly would it still be like Abi-Kardes?

Of course, it was!

We went straight for a meal on Cunda.

I felt Bilal was admiring one of Bilge's cousins.

He started to repeat all the stories about his life and experiences with me when we had lived together in England. Bilge had to advise him to tone down certain bits - as his enthusiasm seemed to make him forget that he was in the company of her parents and family.

He certainly looked the part with longer, blonde hair topping his tanned appearance. Everyone made him so welcome. However, for once he didn't ooze confidence in his usual manner.

I detected something wasn't right.

I later learned that his heart had been broken as Meltem and he had split. Supposedly 'another' was villain.

This break up was so soon after the two of them had been shopping for home comforts for a life together.

I suspected a 'seven-year itch' but this was an opinion not based on fact.

I couldn't offer any criticism of his envisaged fiancé, as she had become a new sister for me over the years and already was considered part of my extended family.

He sought no negative remarks just an outlet for the comfort he needed at this time.

I assured him that she "might well come back".

The sorry tale was left to lie, until the next day.

I questioned Bilal on the beach what a triangular, blue material pack, tied to his bicep with what looked like knicker elastic, meant.

I learned that it hosted selected pages, presumably cuttings, from the Koran (Muslim holy book).

This gesture was apparently a recognised practice at times of extra spiritual need - as this time needed, with him losing his loved one.

Bilge's brother appeared a little overwhelmed, but gossip about people that Bilal knew in the professional game certainly broke the ice and allowed Baba and him to bond with a potential 'intruder'.

Even Bilge was a little slow at forthcoming towards Bilal. His outer facade of confidence, from a person who had such looks, and a life 'on the football stage', could all be somewhat intimidating.

Like me, Bilal, was taken in warmly by my new family.

His short stay was extended, time and time again.

Bilal commented that he really felt that he'd known Baba, Anne, Bilge and Bilen for life.

Suspecting, he was monopolising the conversations and attention, Bilal offered haircare advice to the growing locks of Bilen. Both possessed long hair, though Bilen had more recently decided to grow his. Who's 'ibne' now BA?

In return Baba echoed my advice on Meltem.

Bilge eventually took to him.

It must have taken some getting used to, the apparent bond of eternity, as we joked and laughed as absent friends constantly.

We all went together on family outings, the beach and even shopping trips.

He too, had been adopted.

The commentary was repeated often "that good people find good people" - and bond!

Nearing the end of his stay, we took Bilal to our recently purchased house.

My own home in his land.

All for less than the price of a car in England!

He commented how great a deal we'd struck and said "you'll enjoy Abi, but the real people that will benefit are your children...."

Before his departure, we even took, Bilal and I that is, Baba to a nightclub.

I tried to speak Turkish to the bouncers to gain entry, but Bilal took over in English. Apparently the tourist, presumably with an intended greater spending power, often gained greater access to such venues.

Baba and he had to pretend to be Brits abroad.

He rose and tackled the dance floor - and memories flooded back. Inside he was hurting, but the exterior didn't show such pain.

He gestured for me to join him in the dancing, but I felt somewhat self-conscious.

I was in a nightclub, for the first time, with my 'father-in-law'!

We had a fun time.

On the last night, the men went to watch a Fenerbache match on Digiturk (our equivalent of Sky TV) at a local cafe.

Ortega (the Argentinian playmaker) was awesome.

He'd grace the turf in any Premiership outfit on this display.

We returned to the suburbs of Ayvalik to rendezvous with Hayrettin.

Before departing back to Buca Spor, the Keeper, commented that he'd been surprised how warm this Englishman was contrary to stereotypical perceptions.

He asked me to pass on his regards to Souness (who'd considered him in a coaching role at now Blackburn Rovers), to Brad Friedel, Tugay and Hakan Unsal.

All were together at Galatasaray in former lives.

Souness was clonning a Turkish culture in an ironically heavily populated Muslim Town in Lancashire.

Perhaps he'd been bitten by my bug and love for TURKIYE also?

Bilal ran, and Hayrettin limped, to the bus that was to take them onwards.

We waved goodbye furiously!

But this would not actually be the end, just the beginning of more......

28

Baba and Bilal have swopped mobile telephone numbers and I understand that they have stayed in touch ever since.

SMS text messaging between us all was to increase in volume.....

B appreciated B.

Last SMS message received in 2002, direct to my mobile telephone, was:

"Happy new year my real abi. I hope u and bilge be happy all your life. Your kardes and meltem."

This summer Bilal will marry Meltem.

We all plan to be there.

Finally...a lot of people contributed, in many ways, to the story, either through their suggestions or simply by being there as events unfolded. At all times I have relied upon the all too-fallible human memory in recounting names, places and events that took place.

I have tried to be as precise as I can and recount the stories in as faithful a manner as possible.

In case I missed something, or someone, I apologise in advance. As it has been said before, "The details of the journey may at times change upon recollection, but that does not affect the fact that the journey took place."

My journey did, indeed, take place.

Adrian Stores

Want to know more?

Turkey boasts fantastic tradition, culture and history…and is a great place to visit. The Country spans two continents - Asia and Europe.

Originally from Iran, those who are now known as Turks migrated from Central Asia westwards into Asia Minor towards the end of the 11th Century. They settled there and married the natives. Asia Minor then became known as Turkey after these immigrants. After a while, the religion, Islam, was introduced, as well as the Turks' language, to the Romans and Christians who had earlier resided there.

Laws and customs from bye gone days remain. Men are still conscripted for military service.

The 'half moon' and 'star' of the Turkish flag is to be found everywhere. You might see it on the body of an aeroplane if you fly to the Country with Turkish Airlines.

The story behind the Turkish flag is that the founder of modern Turkey, Kemal Ataturk, chose it. He was a leader of the army during the Turkish War of Independence. When he looked to the sky, he saw a crescent moon and a simple star. The blood of the War, the moon and the star were thus chosen to make up the flag.

Ataturk is a hero in Turkey, he is responsible for many changes that have taken place. Persian and Arabic words were abolished and the alphabet altered to Latin

Scripts. Islam was announced to be a religion and not a lifestyle. Such as the banning of the fez (you may remember the 'Tommy Cooper' hat!) resulted and women were allowed more freedom in what they chose to wear.

The Turkish are warm and friendly people who genuinely want to help visitors. It is common to be referred to as: Abi (brother), Abla (sister), Amca (uncle) or Teyze (aunt) - all as 'a mark of respect'.

More from:

Turkish: A Complete Course for Beginners
(Hodder & Stoughton)
ISBN 0-340-64734-5

Islam
(Hodder & Stoughton)
ISBN 0-340-60901-X

http://www.thy.com

http://www.hotelarcadiaistanbul.com

And a word from Dennis Couniacis:

In this day and age no book would really be complete without a list of useful website addresses.

Lovers of Turkey will find a lot of useful information from the official website at www.turkey.org

For a complete guide to Turkey on the internet you just have to pay www.turkey.com a visit

Galatasary, Turkey's famous football team, is to be found at www.galatasary.com (though Adrian Stores would say I should refer to Fenerbache, Besiktas and probably Kocaelispor to be fairer!).

For a background to Turkey, travelogues and the latest statistics straight from the boffins at C.I.A. headquarters you can no better than an interactive, downloadable Cool Book guide at www.coolpublications.com.

For those who want to find out what's happening in the world of football straight from the source www.fifa.com delivers the goods.

Related titles:

Get Those Sheep Off The Pitch! by Phil Staley
ISBN 0-9543092-0-0

Available from:
www.baa-baa.com and www.amazon.co.uk

GET THOSE SHEEP OFF THE PITCH!

A Life in Non-League Football

by Phil Staley

'Hilarious' Carlo Nash – Manchester City

'A great idea for a terrific book' Tommy Docherty